What people are saying about

Pagan Portals - Thor

Pagan Portals Thor is everything ... It's a concise and solid introduc... ...ty whose mainstream fame has changed t... ...pe of his worship. Morgan Daimler uses clear conversational language to shed light on Thor's ancient myths and legends, while giving practical and modern information for worship now. As a devotee of Thor, I found myself smiling and nodding emphatically through each and every page.

Phoenix Lafae, author or *What Is Remembered Lives*

Morgan Daimler's *Thor* is an incredibly valuable addition to the Pagan Portals series. She takes a figure many readers will feel they know through contemporary popular culture and contextualises him within broader mythology. By doing so, she provides a much more nuanced and intimate portrait of the deity than many of us are accustomed to. Daimler's work feels both authoritative and accessible. The reader is clearly guided through a vast array of texts, whilst also being encouraged to explore ideas further. Alongside this, a number of practical traditions are presented for the reader to incorporate in their practice. By ending each chapter with a more personal reflection on Thor, Daimler helps the reader to prioritise what they have read and develop their own relationship with the deity. This book is a great place to start the journey of meeting Thor.

Andrew Anderson, author of *The Ritual of Writing*

Once again, Ms. Daimler has created a solid guide to exploring the history, mythology, and modern incarnations of an ancient diety. She offers insight into the divinity, symbols, and realities of working with Thor, as well as suggestions of further study and techniques. Her notes on personal experiences with the entity help to bring the scholarship to life and applicable to day-to-day practice.

Christy Nicholas, author of *The Druid's Brooch* Series

Pagan Portals
Thor

Meeting the Norse God of Thunder

Pagan Portals
Thor

Meeting the Norse God of Thunder

Morgan Daimler

**MOON
BOOKS**

Winchester, UK
Washington, USA

JOHN HUNT PUBLISHING

First published by Moon Books, 2020
Moon Books is an imprint of John Hunt Publishing Ltd., No. 3 East Street, Alresford
Hampshire SO24 9EE, UK
office@jhpbooks.net
www.johnhuntpublishing.com
www.moon-books.net

For distributor details and how to order please visit the 'Ordering' section on our website.

Text copyright: Morgan Daimler 2019

ISBN: 978 1 78904 115 6
978 1 78904 116 3 (ebook)
Library of Congress Control Number: 2019942146

A CIP catalogue record for this book is available from the British Library.

Design: Stuart Davies

UK: Printed and bound by CPI Group (UK) Ltd, Croydon, CR0 4YY
US: Printed and bound by Thomson-Shore, 7300 West Joy Road, Dexter, MI 48130

We operate a distinctive and ethical publishing philosophy in
all areas of our business, from our global network of authors to
production and worldwide distribution.

Contents

This book is dedicated to my hetero life partner
Melody Legaspi-Seils, our level 7 friendship, and the day
we met (even if neither of us can remember the story).

Author's Note

Pagan Portals is a series whose purpose is to offer people a solid introduction to specific topics. This book is intended to serve as such an introduction to the Norse God, Thor, giving a reader a basic overview of his history, mythology, symbols, and his presence in the modern world. It would be impossible in a book this small to cover any of these topics fully so what we will do here is aim to touch on each of them in a way that gives readers a grounding in the topic. Those who want to go further can look at the bibliography for suggested further reading.

In writing this book I have tried to find a balance between academic sources and personal experiences. As someone who has been part of the Heathen community for over a decade I want to share my own experience honouring Thor so that people can see at least one possible expression of Heathenry in the modern world, but I also want to provide a strong academic resource for readers. I have tried to include an extensive bibliography and list a selection of other references that could potentially help readers connect to Thor in both intellectual and experiential ways.

As with my previous books I am using American Psychological Association (APA) formatting for citations which means that after any quoted or paraphrased material you will see a set of parenthesis containing the author's last name and the date the book was published; this can be cross-referenced in the bibliography if you would like to know the source. I realize not everyone likes this style but I prefer it because I find it the most efficient way to reference sources.

It would be impossible to include everything about Thor in a single book of this size, however, I have tried to include what I consider the most pertinent information. Ideally readers will be interested enough to continue researching and reading more, but if this is the only book on Thor that you read it should still give you a solid basic understanding of who Thor was and is. To accomplish this I am looking at sources spanning both Norse and Germanic cultures, historic and modern, as well as books about Thor written by scholars as well as non-academics who feel a strong connection to him. I believe that this wide approach is the only way to get a true understanding of Thor fully in context.

This book by nature will likely tend to focus on a more Heathen perspective, both historic and modern, but it is written for anyone interested in Thor regardless of religion or belief system. I realize that this may be something of a contentious approach because some modern practitioners of pagan faiths like Wicca and Asatru can be a bit antagonistic but I would rather cast a wide net than be overly specific in the audience I write for. I don't think that a person's religion matters as much as the intent with which they approach the Gods and the effort they put into learning about them and connecting to them. So, whether you are a Heathen, Asatruar, Reconstructionist, Neo-pagan, Wiccan, witch or any other variety of pagan or polytheist this book should still be useful to you. That said, however, my own personal experiences will tend to be framed within the context of my spirituality as an American Heathen with Reconstructionist tendencies.

Introduction

If you ask a random person to name a God from the Norse pantheon the first name that most people will mention is Thor. His modern fame likely owes a great deal to pop-culture but historically we see that Thor has long been a well-known and beloved deity, the God of the common man as opposed to the nobility. So important was Thor to the pagan Norse that the Norse settlers in Dublin, Ireland, were known by the Irish as *'muintir Tomar'* or *'Thor's people'* and our modern English name for Thursday comes from his name, literally 'Thor's Day'. It should be no surprise then that he has continued to be an influence in Paganism and Heathenry today and that many people still look to Thor for protection and guidance in their lives.

There is abundant evidence for a cult of Thor during the pagan period, not only because of the place names and statues in temples, but also because of engraving on rune stones, personal names, and references to Thor's worship in texts. There are at least four known runestones carved with notes asking for Thor's blessing as well as more with Thor's Hammers carved into them which are believed to serve the same purpose as the written inscriptions (Simek, 1983). We find Thor used as part of a variety of different names in the sagas including the seeress Thordis. Þórólfur Mostrarskegg in the Eyrbyggja Saga took his name from Thor, who he considered to be his special patron, and according to the story his faith in Thor was so strong that when he came to Iceland to settle he took the high seat pillars from his temple and threw them overboard as the ship approached shore, asking that Thor guide them to the best place to land. Supporting the idea of an active cult to Thor during the pagan period we see not only all of the above but also references in the texts to sacrifices made to Thor and to a belief in some of the dead potentially going to Thor's hall in the afterlife (Simek, 1993). There is also evidence of an oath ring of Thor that may have been kept in temples where Thor was worshipped (Ellis Davidson, 1964).

Temples and shrines during the Heathen period often included Thor, and his images are more often described in historic accounts than any others. Some of these temples had their statue of Thor in a wagon pulled by intricately carved goats, and by at least one account this entire object could be pulled by a rope attached to the goats, which Ellis Davidson theorizes may have been part of a ritual to Thor. We have a recorded instance of the Christian Olaf Tryggvason being tricked into pulling this cord, and when he is then told he has *done a service* to the Norse God he has his men destroy the shrine while he personally knocks down Thor's statue (Ellis Davidson, 1964). This reinforces Thor's significance as well as the tension of the conversion period. There's also one later reference to a temple of Thor that may have had a perpetual flame burning on the altar (Ellis Davidson, 1964). The statues might also be made to hold hammers, replicas of Thor's hammer, Mjolnir, and the temple might have other such hammers on hand as sacred items. These temple hammers were made of bronze according to an account by Saxo Grammaticus and might possibly have been used to imitate the sound of thunder for some ritual purpose (Ellis Davidson, 1964).

In modern English his name has been Anglicized to Thor. He was called Þórr or Þunarr in Old Norse, Þunor in Anglo-Saxon, Þunar in West Germanic, and Donar in Old High German; Thor's name means thunder rather than the more usual interpretation given of thunderer (Simek, 1993). This can sometimes cause confusion in trying to understand if a certain piece of folklore or saying is attributed to Thor or one of his cognates because of the linguistic ambiguity. He is often compared to other thunder deities, particularly Taranis, Jupiter, Jove, Zeus, and Hercules although it is best to understand him within his own context.

During the conversion period when the Norse were moving to Christianity Thor became the main adversarial deity of the

Heathens in opposition to the Christians. In Njal's Saga there's mention of a belief that Thor challenged Christ to a fight which the Christian God dared not accept while an account from Norway depicts him in a one-on-one contest with God's champion (the Christian king of Norway of course), showing perhaps how contentious the duelling beliefs were. During this same period Christian crosses and Thor's Hammer pendants were often cast in the same mould as followers of each religion sought a symbol to wear that would show their alignment clearly and jewellers struggled to keep up with the demand. As Turville-Petre so eloquently said:

> "To the end, Thor was the defender of the pagan world, the world of gods (Asgard)." (Turville-Petre, 1993, page 89).

His popularity has also been strong during the modern Heathen revival, although arguably perhaps not as strong as during the original Heathen period. During the original Heathen period and into the conversion period there is ample evidence that Thor was considered a primary deity. For example 25% of the people named in the Landnámbók have names that incorporate Thor's name, while very few other deity names are found as part of personal names (Turville-Petre, 1964). In the modern era, as people are converting back to Heathenry, the worship of the Gods is not identical to what it was, with a more diverse focus and different understandings of who and what the Gods were. Thor is also not viewed as a pre-eminent deity of every aspect of human life anymore by many new Heathens but rather his purviews are narrowed down to a smaller range.

When we look at Thor today we find an often misunderstood or underestimated deity, so part of the goal of this Pagan Portal is not only to introduce people to Thor but also to dig into his history and mythology and unravel the truth behind the hammer-wielding hero many think they know. We will be looking at

Thor's personal connections among the other Gods, his place in mythology, his appearances outside Norse and Icelandic stories, his possessions, and building on that to look at his place in the modern world and ways to connect to him. While we will only be able to cover so much in a book of this size hopefully it will serve as a solid basic introduction and a good starting place to study further.

Chapter 1

Who is Thor?

Thor is a deity who is in many ways a contradiction, a God who is often described as almost oafish, yet who defeats a dwarf named Alviss (All-wise) in a battle of wits, a God who fights giants and forces of entropy in his myths yet who also blesses brides at weddings and is called on to ensure the fertility of people and crops. While some modern views of him can be shallow, in truth he is a complex and multi-faceted deity who deserves an in-depth study to truly be understood.

Part of the key to understanding this complexity is accepting that there are aspects of Thor that are contradictory, perhaps formed across the centuries of belief, but that these contradictions don't cancel each other out. Thor can be quick tempered and direct and still be clever and canny in different situations; just as he may seem to be duped in some stories (often by magical means) yet can also hold his own in a battle of wits and even come out victorious through a genuinely devious plan. We must understand in looking at Thor that he is not a one dimensional being but multi-layered and take each layer for its own significance.

Thor was definitely one of the most popular deities in the Norse cultures with his name found in various place-names and references to his image in major temples. In the Gesta Hammaburgensis ecclesiae pontificum, Adam of Bremen describes the temple at Upsala Sweden this way:

"...the images of three gods are worshipped by the people. As the mightiest of them, Thor has his throne in the middle of the room; the places on either side of him are taken by Woden [Odin] and Fricco [Freyr]" (Adam of Bremen, 1876).

This central placement emphasizes Adam's words that Thor was *'the mightiest of them'*. It's possible that Adam here means mightiest in terms of strength but he may also have meant mightiest by his popularity. Certainly that would explain his central placement in the temple better than an emphasis on physical prowess. As Turville-Petre describes him in reference to the late Heathen period in 'Myth and Religion of the North':

> *"Thor was admired most by those among whom tradition was the strongest....He was wise, mighty, and brave, incorporating the ideals of his worshippers...he was the enemy of evil, chaotic giants."* (Turville-Petre, 1964, page 92).

Thor was well loved by the people, enough so that he was worshipped through the conversion period and into the end of the Heathen period, even having a solid place among the Norse in Dublin in the 11th century (Ellis Davidson, 1964). This is not to say that other Gods weren't also acknowledged, because they certainly were, most especially Freyr, Odin, and Njord, but Thor held a special place among the Heathen Norse. His personality, bravery, and straightforward fighting made him a symbol of the ultimate Viking age hero (Ellis Davidson, 1964).

Thor's Appearance

Thor is often described in mythology with red hair and a beard; many older artistic depictions follow the lead of mythology. In Flóamanna Saga Thor appeared to a man who had converted to Christianity as a large red-bearded man (Ellis Davidson, 1964). In modern depictions Thor is sometimes viewed as a blonde although there's not as much evidence for this as for Thor with red hair. People who dispute Thor as a blonde often point to Marvel Comics as a source, however, Snorri Sturluson in the prologue to the Prose Edda describes Thor with *"hair...lovelier than gold"*[1] although it must be kept in mind this is the most heavily euhemerized portion of that text. It's also possible in this case red gold was being referred to.

He is seen as a man of great strength and size, with an enormous appetite. There are several accounts of Thor as a guest among giants devouring entire cows, more than a half dozen salmon, and trenchers of mead. This indomitable appetite is as much a part of Thor as his physical strength or red beard, symbolizing his larger than life vitality. His great physical strength is often emphasized in stories and we see it being utilized to his advantage when he doesn't have his hammer with him. For example, in the story of Thor and the giant, Geirrod, Thor must use his strength to fight back against Geirrod's two daughters when they attack him by lifting him up and trying to crush him against the ceiling.

Thor travels either by riding in a goat drawn chariot or by walking. This may be because he was too big for a horse to carry him, although it's also possible that the symbolism is related to class. If horses were the means of travel for the upper classes then it would be logical for Thor, god of the common man, to walk or ride in a chariot pulled by goats. Its also worth noting here that when Thor journeys he is sometimes accompanied by a human which likely also represents his close ties to humanity.

There is also at least one story, the account of Thor's battle with the giant, Hrungnir, which says that Thor has part of a whetstone embedded in his head. This happened as the two fought and Thor threw Mjolnir at Hrungnir who held up a whetstone to defend himself; the hammer smashed the stone before killing the giant. According to the story this is how whetstones ended up in earthly quarries, as the shrapnel fell to our world, while a single piece lodged in Thor's head (Crossley-Holland, 1980). This is a seemingly odd story but Ellis Davidson suggests that it may reflect older ritual practices, perhaps an initiation re-enacting the combat, and also possibly may have been used to explain the source of lightning. She notes a Laplander practice

9

of starting fires with the head of a thunder deity, and relates the idea of metal hitting the embedded whetstone to steel striking flint (Ellis Davidson, 1964).

Thor's Family

Throughout the mythology Thor is said to be the son of Odin, and according to Snorri his first son (Simek, 1993; Lindow, 2001). Odin is established as the head of the pantheon, a god of kings and poets in contrast to Thor's patronage of the common man. It is difficult to characterize Thor's relationship with his father based on the mythology, but we could perhaps say it is amicable if slightly uneasy. In the Hárbarðsljóð the two engage in a flyting with each other, which is something like an insult battle although in that case Thor doesn't seem to know it is Odin he is speaking to. In the story of Thor's battle with the giant, Hrungnir, when Thor gives the giant's horse to his son Magni, Odin complains that it should have been given to him instead. Both of these examples might indicate a more contentious relationship between them but there's no other indication of that elsewhere and otherwise Thor seems to act to defend the Aesir and uphold the community his father has established and leads. Odin in at least two cases – when Hrungnir arrives in Asgard and when Loki crashes Aegir's feast – relies on Thor to restore peace and order to the situation.

Through his father he has many half-brothers, although mythology is often contradictory about exactly who Odin's other children are. We can certainly say that Thor's half-brothers would include Baldur and Vali, and perhaps Heimdall, Tyr, Bragi, Vidar[2], and Hodur as well. Baldur doesn't appear in any stories directly with Thor but Thor is noted in the story of Baldur's funeral. Heimdall also doesn't play a large role with Thor in most stories although he is the one in the Thrymskvida who suggests the plan for Thor to get his hammer back. Tyr is said to be one of Thor's travelling companions in several of the stories.

Thor's mother is the goddess Jord (literally 'earth') also sometimes alternately named Fjorgyn (also 'earth') or Hlodyn (meaning unknown). These three names are usually understood to be alternate terms for the same being, all different versions of a name for the goddess of the earth (Simek, 1993). According to Snorri Sturluson, in the Prose Edda Thor's mother is counted among the Goddesses of the Aesir (Young, 1964). This is worth noting as people today do refer to Thor as the son of a giantess, which he may in truth be, but his mother was considered one of the Aesir according to at least this source and there was usually a difference in how a being was related to depending on which group they were considered part of.

Thor's Wife and Mistress

Thor had a wife among the Aesir and also had a lover among the giants. This may seem strange to us today because of current mores but the idea of a person having a legal spouse as well as concubines or lovers was within the norm under certain circumstances in Norse culture at different times. When we look at Thor's relationships they should be understood in this context.

Thor's wife is the goddess Sif, renowned for her beautiful golden hair, which after being shorn and then replaced by Loki, was literally made from gold which grew like real hair. Her name is of uncertain meaning but may possibly relate to the word for wife (Simek, 1993). Simek discusses the lack of evidence for any cult relating to Sif in his 'Dictionary of Northern Mythology' although many modern Heathens have given Sif a role as an agricultural, and specifically harvest, goddess. Ellis Davidson in 'Gods and Myths of Northern Europe' takes the opposite view to Simek, suggesting the possibility that Sif's golden hair might represent ripe fields of grain and that she may have been a goddess of fertility although this is never stated as fact.

Thor's lover among the giants, with whom he has a child, Magni, is the giantess Járnsaxa. Her name means *'the one with the iron knife'* and she is also mentioned in the list of nine giantesses who were mother to Heimdall (Simek, 1993; Lindow, 2001). Little is known about her beyond a small number of references to her name in a few stories. In the Skáldskaparmál Sif is called *"one who shares a man with Járnsaxa"* (Lindow, 2001).

Thor's Children

Thor has two sons named Magni and Modi and one daughter named Thrúd, as well as one step-son named Ullr. The giantess Járnsaxa is Magni's mother and it is implied, but uncertain, that Sif is the mother of the other two. Mythology states that after the final battle of the Gods, Magni and Modi will inherit their father's hammer, and one might assume his protective role. In Thor's battle with the giant, Hrungnir, Magni, although only a small child, is the only one strong enough to free Thor from underneath the giant's body. There is no surviving mythology about Modi, although we are told in the Völuspú that he will survive the doom of the Gods.

There is very little known about Thor's daughter Thrúd. She does not appear directly in any stories so we only know of her from references to her in other stories and from by-names of other beings. For example Thor is also known by the kenning 'Father of Thrúd' and the giant, Hrungnir, is called 'Thief of Thrúd' in the Ragnarsdrápa, although we know nothing of any story which may have explained that name (Lindow, 2001).

Simek suggests that all three children are personified aspects of Thor himself, representing his strength in the case of Magni and Thrud, whose names are words for strength, and his temper in the case of Modi whose name is related to the concept of anger.

Thor and Loki

It's impossible to write about Thor's family and not also add a note about his most common travelling partner, the mischievous deity Loki. Although we do have some stories of Thor adventuring alone or with Tyr or Thjálfi in many of his tales he is accompanied by Loki. Their relationship, like Loki's relationship with many of the Gods more generally, is an ambivalent one with many stories seeming to depict them as friends while others show them in a more contentious light.

Loki is the child of the giant Farbauti and the giantess Laufey, married to the Goddess Sigyn with whom he had two sons, and also lover of the giantess Angrboda with whom he has three dangerous children: the Midgard serpent Jormungandr, the Fenris wolf, and the goddess Hel. Because of Loki's changeable nature he is also the mother of the eight legged horse Sleipnir[3]. He is counted among the Aesir by Snorri in the Gylfaginning and is called Odin's blood-brother in the Lokasenna. For the bulk of Norse myth he acts as a friend to the Gods although his motivations are often as much self-preservation as altruism. He causes as many problems as he solves. Only at the end of the narrative arc of the myths does he become an enemy to the Aesir and act against them by engineering Baldur's death and ensuring that he cannot be brought back from Helheim[4] and we are told in the Völuspú that he will ride out against the Aesir with the army of the dead.

There is some implication that Loki may also have been the lover of Thor's wife, Sif, something that is never directly shown in any story but which Loki claims is true in the Lokasenna. In that story Loki has arrived at a gathering of the Aesir uninvited and begun insulting each person present, following a pattern of insulting a person then another intervening to defend the first, at which Loki moves on to insult that person. Towards the end of this Sif approaches him and pours him a drink, claiming that he has no insult to offer he, knowing that she is blameless. He replies:

"Alone thou wert if truly thou wouldst
All men so shyly shun;
But one do I know full well, methinks,
Who had thee from [Thor's] arms,--
Loki the crafty in lies."
(Bellows, 1936)

Similarly, in the Hárbarðsljóð, Odin, in disguise, tells Thor that Sif has a lover back home while Thor is out travelling. There has been some speculation that this may be Loki's motivation for cutting off Sif's hair in another story, something that was culturally significant as a sign of a loss of honour.

Thjálfi

Another person who should be mentioned here is the human Thjálfi who sometimes accompanies Thor on his journeys. Thjálfi and his sister are the children of farmers who Thor stayed with; one of Thor's goats was accidently lamed by the boy and in punishment for the offense Thor took both Thjálfi and his sister as servants. Thjálfi is a swift runner and is often referred to in stories as the fastest runner, a skill that comes in handy and that may hint at more than mortal origins. It's possible though that Thor's human travelling companion is a symbol of the God's close connections to humankind (Lindow, 2001).

Thor's Adversaries

As important as it is to discuss Thor's family and allies we cannot understand without discussing Thor's main adversaries in the mythology because understanding who Thor stands against tells us a great deal about him. Thor is often depicted as a hot-tempered God but he never kills without reason or motivation and he can show a great deal of restraint when necessary. His usual enemies are those who ultimately either seek to bring chaos to the worlds or who are actively endangering it, undoubtedly why he earned the name 'protector of humankind' although he is just as essential to protecting the Gods. On several occasions we see Thor's arrival sending a threat fleeing, or even just the threat of Thor's anger; in the Lokasenna when Loki has offended all the Gods and is refusing to leave the feasting hall it is only Thor's threats against him that finally get him to leave, as he says:

"But before thee alone, do I now go forth, For thou fightest well..." (Bellows, 1936 page 175).

The idea of Thor's battle prowess intimidating his enemies is also seen in the Hyndluljóð where Freya is negotiating with the giantess, Hyndla, and she offers to make offerings to Thor that Hyndla will be protected from him.

Sometimes people have the idea that Thor is a simple giant killer but the reality is more nuanced than that; it is true that Thor in the stories is a killer of giants but not only giants and not all giants. Thor also has allies among the giants, including Jarnsaxa who is the mother of one of his sons, and also Gríd who gives him his iron gloves and belt. The main giants that Thor was opposed to were the more destructive and dangerous beings, those that had a reputation for doing great harm, or those who were threatening Asgard, the domain of the Gods. He is also an equal opportunity giant killer, fighting both male and female giants.

Jormungandr, the Midgard serpent, is one of Thor's most important adversaries in the myths although the two rarely meet in stories. Lindow in 'Norse Mythology' explains this important antipathy by the fact that the Midgard serpent, although in the form of a great snake or dragon, is actually a giant, as Lindow puts it *"the most powerful giant of all"* (Lindow, 2001, page 287). It is perfectly logical then that the most powerful God would be pitted against the most powerful giant in such a vital struggle.

Thor and the Midgard serpent are important opponents in several stories, including the seeress's prediction of Ragnarök. Jormungandr is a child of Loki and the giantess Angrboda, sibling to the goddess, Hel, and the Fenris wolf. Jormungandr's name is related to the word for earth (Simek, 1993). The Midgard serpent is one of several monstrous serpents found in Norse myth alternately described as great snakes or dragons although Jormungandr is usually understood to be some kind of legless snakelike creature.

In one story of Thor's travels where he encounters the giant Utgard-Loki, Thor engages in a competition where he is challenged to lift a cat off the ground, only the cat is actually the Midgard serpent in disguise. Thor is able to shift the animal although not fully lift it but even that speaks to his immense strength.

In another story which dates to the 9th and 10th centuries Thor visits the giant, Hymir, and the two go fishing during which Thor hooks Jormungandr and pulls the great serpent to the surface (Simek, 1993). There are different versions of this story, some of which suggest Thor killed the serpent either when he lifted it from the water or as it was being dropped back in but there are also versions where the serpent escaped alive.

In the final confrontation between the Aesir and the forces of entropy at Ragnarök, Thor will battle against the Midgard serpent. This fight will be their ultimate battle, with Jormungandr wounding Thor and Thor finally killing the serpent. However, after the battle Thor will die, either from his wounds or from poison from the wounds. Since many of the one on one fights described by the seeress in this battle seem to represent the confrontation of opposing forces, this may perhaps indicate that Thor and the Midgard serpent are such a pairing. Simek feels that the adversarial relationship between the two may reflect both an older Indo-European motif of a God struggling against a monster as well as show later Christian influence[5].

In the same vein as Thor's giant killing he is also said to kill other dangerous beings including trolls. When Thor is travelling in the mythology he is sometimes journeying into the world of giants but he is also said to go out to battle trolls 'in the east' (Lindow, 2001). In folklore from several Norse countries it is said that Thor would ride through the sky during thunderstorms hurling stones down at trolls on earth.

Additionally, although more rarely, Thor kills dwarves. We have a couple accounts of this in the Eddas, one intentionally although not using physical force and the other in a fit of grief (Lindow, 2001). In the Alvissmal Thor delays the dwarf, Alviss, who has come seeking his daughter in marriage until the sun rises and the dwarf is turned to stone. In the story of Baldur's death Thor is so grief stricken at his brother's funeral, and so enraged at the giantess who refused to weep and bring Baldur back to life, that he kicks the dwarf, Lit, into the funeral pyre. We might not then consider dwarves adversaries of Thor in the way that giants or trolls would be.

It must also be noted that during the conversion period Thor was seen to be the main adversary of the Christian God with several examples in the sagas of missionaries claiming their God was mightier than Thor and the Heathens in turn claiming that Thor was the more powerful. For example in one part of Erik the Red's Saga the Heathen, Thorhall, has prayed to Thor before he and his Christian companions find a whale on the beach. Thorhall then declares:

"Redbeard [Thor] has got the better of your Christ! I have done this by my poetry which I made about Thor, in whom men trust." (Ellis Davidson, 1964, page 85).

Similarly in Njal's Saga there is a conversation between a missionary and a Heathen woman who says that it is Thor who has wrecked the man's ship, and claims that Thor has challenged the Christian God to a fight but he is too scared of the Thunder God to do it. This illustrates the contentious attitude that pervaded the conversion area in some places and belief that the Gods themselves were grappling with each other and were interfering with each other's followers. It also demonstrates the belief that Thor, of all the Gods, was best equipped to take on the looming threat represented by Christian missionaries. Just as Thor was the defender of Asgard and the human world from giants and forces of entropy, so he was seen by the Heathens of the period as the ideal one to defend the Gods against the encroaching danger of the new religion (Turville-Petre, 1964).

The two were often described as Red Thor and White Christ but this terminology has deeper layers than may at first be obvious. Red was associated both with having red hair, as one might assume, and also with fierceness, stubbornness, and might while white was associated with cowardice and weakness as well as literally paleness (Gundarsson, 2006). Calling Thor 'Red Thor' then had connotations of Thor's strength and battle prowess and calling Christ white implied his weakness in alignment with the wider Heathen dialogue which placed Thor as the stronger and more ready to fight. Eventually Heathenry did give way before the new religion but it is clear from the evidence that the changeover was not easy or without contention and that Thor was the main Heathen deity seen in opposition to Christianity.

Other Names for Thor

The Norse Gods all have various by-names or kennings which are poetic names they were also known by. Some have many more than others but we do know of several that were applied to Thor:

Hlorithi – uncertain meaning, a name used for Thor in the
Lokasenna and Hymiskvida
Hafra dróttin – 'lord of the goats' a name for Thor in the

Hymiskvida

Hafra njótr – 'user of goats' a name for Thor in the Húsdrápa

Reidar Tyr – 'Wagon God' name for Thor in the Skáldskaparmál

Ása-Thor – 'Thor of the Aesir' a name used for Thor in the Prose Edda

Protector of humans – kenning for Thor in the Hymiskvida

Slayer of the Serpent – another kenning for Thor found in the Hymiskvida

Ving-Thor – a name for Thor in the Alvissmal. It may mean 'Thor the Hallower' although that is hypothetical (Turville-Petre, 1964).

Þórr karl – literally 'old man Thor'

Father of Thrud – a kenning for Thor in the Skáldskaparmál

Father of Modi – another name for Thor from the Skáldskaparmál

Husband of Sif - another name for Thor from the Skáldskaparmál

Son of Jord – a name that Thor is called in several different sources

Orms einbani – 'lone killer of the serpent', a name referencing Thor killing the Midgard serpent found in the Hymiskvida

Thor in My Life

Thor was one of the first Norse gods that I learned about, in part because he's so well-known and in part because he's so well loved in modern Heathenry. When I was new to Heathenry I started out by reading the Poetic and Prose Eddas and while I was immediately drawn to Odin personally it's hard not to develop a fondness for Thor throughout the stories. He appears in many of the tales and while he does have a temper he is also both a protector of human-kind and a surprisingly nuanced character.

My initial understanding of Thor was, I must admit, shallow and heavily influenced by the way that I saw him being discussed in the modern Heathen community around me. Thor tended to be relegated to a couple narrow depictions, either the friendly big brother or the macho warrior with little shading in between. Of course, there were a few people that were closer to Thor, who had developed deeper practices around him or fuller dedication – what Heathens call 'fulltrui' – that did seem to understand Thor differently but they were less vocal than the others. Understandable since their relationships with Thor were more personal. Because of this, though, my own view of him was undeniably limited and unfairly so. It wasn't until I really delved into who Thor was and the meaning he had held for the older Heathens that I began to see different sides to Thor. Yes he can have that big brother energy and that warrior energy to him, but he can also be a leader, oath-taker, consecrator, and bringer of abundance. I re-read his stories very differently later on when my view of him had shifted away from the simpler ideas and even now I find new layers to some of his stories when I give them a fresh read.

As I was beginning my journey into Heathenry I found it only natural to include Thor, or his German counterpart Donar, on my altar and in my worship. While I have drifted away from honouring him over time as my focus has shifted more solidly to the Huldufolk (in various cultural manifestations) I am still fond of him and will still say 'Hail Thor' during thunder storms in appreciation for both his presence and his protection over the earth.

End Notes

1   Quote from Young, 1964, page 25.

2   Interestingly Vidar's mother, the giantess Gird, is helpful to Thor on one of his adventures when he needed to confront a dangerous giant without the aid of his hammer Mjolnir. Although Thor has a reputation for killing giants it should be noted that not all giants were enemies of the Gods and some

were helpful to them. Thor did not kill indiscriminately and clearly did have some allies among the giant folk.

3 Sleipnir is Odin's particular steed and able to travel between the nine worlds. He is the product of Loki and the stallion Svadilfari, whose conception was brought about after Loki was forced to distract the horse which was helping a giant build a wall around Asgard. Loki had encouraged the Aesir to enter into a bet with the giant that he could not finish the wall within a certain amount of time or the Aesir would give him the sun, moon, and goddess Freya. When it looked like the giant would succeed at his task the Aesir pressured Loki into interfering to ensure the giant would fail, which Loki did by luring the stallion away so that the giant was unable to move the stones he needed to finish the construction.

4 There is a possibility that even this action though is done, ultimately, to benefit the Gods as this ensures that Baldur is spared the fate of the other Aesir during Ragnarok. This places him in a position to return and take up his role again in the new world that arises after the old is destroyed, something that would be impossible if he were present during the final battle.

It is also worth noting as an aside that the Norse Helheim is largely unlike the Christian Hell despite the borrowed the name. So Baldur is not suffering during the interim but rather is described as an honoured guest feasting in the hall where most of the ancestors go after death.

5 See Simek 'Dictionary of Northern Mythology' pages 324 – 325 for more on this.

Chapter 2

Thor in Mythology

Thor appears across a wide array of mythology, a testament to both his popularity and his role as a defender of order against chaos. Reading the various sources allows us to understand Thor from the perspective of the conversion period and immediate post-conversion period, but it is important to remember that these stories only give us a portion of who Thor is. A lot of material has been lost in the last thousand years, as demonstrated by the number of references we have in the existing stories to other incidence or tales that we now know nothing about. There is also no way to know how much once existed in folk belief that was never written down in any form or would have been virtually unknown to the literati of the time.

We must also contend with the undeniable fact that while much of the material we do have was recorded very close to the end of the Heathen period it was still written by Christians. There is no way to know what bias this may have brought to the stories or how they may have been subtly changed.

All of this said it does not mean that the mythology has no value to us today, in fact the recorded myths are a vital cornerstone along with later surviving folk beliefs, archaeological evidence, and modern evolutions in belief. Thor is more than just who he was 1,000 years ago but in order to fully understand him we must strive to understand who he was in the myths and how he appeared in stories written by people living during a time when Heathen belief had not fully died out.

What follows is as many of the places that Thor appears in the myths and sagas as I was able to find, although I am only able to summarize these appearances here. I suggest that readers look to the original material for a fuller picture, especially the Prose and Poetic Eddas and a good modern retelling like Crossley-Holland's 'Norse Myths'. This chapter can serve as a good jumping off point to find the full versions of the stories if you want, otherwise it should give you a basic grasp of how Thor was depicted across the older literature.

The Prose Edda

Written by Snorri Sturluson around the 12th century, the Prose Edda is a collection of stories about the Norse Gods, framed as a narrative between a man named Gylfi and the God, Odin. It begins, as many such texts do, by euhemerizing the Aesir, claiming that they are not Gods but humans who came from Troy in Turkey. Thor appears early in this euhemeristic prologue where Snorri tries to establish that he was actually the grandson of Priam, the king of Troy[1], educated in Thrace, who journeyed out and fought giants and monsters. Snorri describes this mortal Thor marrying a woman named Sybil who he claims the Icelanders called Sif and then traces his descendants down seventeen generations to Odin (also a mortal in this prologue) who was a seer and gifted in magic; Odin set out and journeyed north to what would be Germany, Sweden, and Norway where he established kingdoms.

This prologue gives way immediately to a more clearly pagan storytelling, with the beginning of the Prose Edda telling of how Gylfi, the king of Sweden, came to lose a portion of his land to the Goddess, Gefjon, after agreeing to give her whatever portion of land she could plough in a day and night. Gefjon harnessed four oxen who were actually her sons by a giant for this endeavour and they ploughed so deeply the land was cut away creating the island of Zealand. Having then established the tone going forward Snorri tells of Gylfi journeying to Asgard, the home of the Gods, and having a conversation about cosmology and theology with Odin disguised as High, Just-As-High, and Third.

During the conversation Odin talks to Gylfi about Thor,

describing him as both the strongest of the Gods and the most important. He says that Thor's home is called Thrúðvangar and his hall is named Bilskirnir, and he talks about several of Thor's possessions including his goats and hammer.

He also relates a story about the building of Asgard's walls where a giant tried to make a deal with the Gods to win the sun, moon, and Freya by swearing to build a wall around the Gods' domain within a specific amount of time. Loki convinced the Gods to agree but when it looked as if the giant would succeed Loki was forced to intervene, distracting the builder's horse so that he ran off and the giant failed to meet his goal. After this Thor returned from his travels and attacked the giant, killing him.

Later he tells another story of Thor's travels. In that tale Thor and Loki are journeying and stop for the night at a farmstead. As is his custom Thor slaughters his two goats and put the meat and bones in a cauldron, laying the skin out nearby. He invited the farmer and his family to share the meal asking that they throw the bones onto the skins as they ate. The farmer's son Thjálfi split one of the leg bones to suck out the marrow, and when Thor used his hammer to resurrect the goats the next morning one was lame because of that. In punishment Thor takes the two children to be his servants and, leaving the goats behind, he, Loki, and the two children go on to Jotunheim, the land of giants. Once there they stumble across something they think is a large hall and spend the night in it, only to be tormented by strange noises and rumblings all night long. Upon waking the group find an enormous giant outside, who introduces himself as 'Skrýmir' [big one] and tells them they have slept the night in his glove. He asks if they would like to travel with him for a ways and they agree, however, it does not go well with Skrýmir tying their food in a bag none of them can open. Thor tries three times to strike him with Mjolnir but each time the giant seems oblivious to the blows. He advises them as they part ways that they are approaching the fort of Utgarð-Loki who he warns is a powerful and dangerous giant. When the group arrives at Utgarð-Loki's hall they are challenged to prove their individual skills: Loki in an eating contest, Thjálfi in a foot race, and Thor in a drinking contest, contest of strength, and wrestling match. They each lose. Only when they are leaving the stronghold does Utgarð-Loki confess that he has deceived them with magic from the beginning to protect his stronghold from Thor's strength. Skrýmir was actually Utgarð-Loki and he tied the provision bag with iron to keep Thor from opening it; he also deceived Thor's sight so that his hammer blows fell on a hill rather the giants head, sparing him. Loki lost an eating contest against fire itself, while Thjálfi lost his race to thought. Thor's drinking horn was filled with the ocean, impossible to drain; the cat he failed to lift off the ground was actually the Midgard Serpent; the old woman he lost a wrestling match to was time. Hearing all this revealed Thor was furious but when he turned to strike Utgarð-Loki the giant and his fort had disappeared.

The next story of Thor tells of how he sought out the Midgard serpent to try to redeem his embarrassment over failing to lift the creature previously. He went fishing with a giant named Hymir, rowing far out seeking the serpent that is wrapped around the earth. When the serpent bit on his line he lifted it from the water, meaning to kill it, but Hymir panicked at the sight and cut the line. Some say Thor killed the serpent then anyway, according to Snorri, but others that the serpent escaped that day.

Thor is briefly mentioned later during a story about the pursuit and capture of Loki for his part in Baldur's death. Loki turns himself in a salmon to hide in a river but the Aesir tracked him down. A net was cast to try to catch him; Thor held a rope attached to the end. After two failed attempts to drag him out Loki tried to jump free and Thor managed to catch his fish-form by the tail which is why they say the salmon's tail is shaped the way that it is.

His final appearance in the Prose Edda is in the retelling of the prediction of Ragnarok, where it's said he will have one final confrontation with the Midgard serpent:

"Thor will slay the Midgard serpent but stagger back only nine paces before he falls down dead, on account of the poison blown on him by the serpent."[2] (Young, 1964, page 88).

The Poetic Edda

The Poetic Edda is a collection of poems by anonymous authors gathered around the 13th century. The poems vary in nature and tone, from comedic to serious to apocalyptic. Thor features in many of them and it would be beyond the scope of this book to recap each poem but I will highlight some of the more important or well-known stories found in this collection.

Hárbarðsljóð is another narrative poem that focuses largely on Thor. It is written as flyting, a style of text that involves an exchange of insults between two speakers. In this story Thor has been out travelling alone when he comes to a river that cannot be crossed without the aid of a ferry; the ferryman is resting on the opposite shore. Thor hails him and asks for a ride across only to receive a rude response and so begins a series of back and forth between the two. The ferryman is actually Odin in disguise as Harbard [grey beard] and he uses this situation to challenge Thor's activities and preference for defending the common man, insulting him by insinuating that Thor is a peasant himself and of ill reputation. There's also some entertaining interplay between them as they each brag of their deeds, with Thor emphasizing his exploits killing giants and Odin his success with women.

Hymiskvida is the next major story which features Thor. In this poem the Aesir are going to attend a feast at Aegir's home but Aegir says he needs a cauldron to accomplish the preparations. Thor and Tyr set off together to get the cauldron after Tyr suggests they go to the giant, Hymir,[3] and get his which is 'a league deep'

(Larrington, 1996). Thor does not prove a particularly good house guest, breaking eight other cauldrons and eating two whole cows; this latter action prompts Hymir to suggest the two of them go hunting the next day to which Thor in turn suggests fishing instead. The interval that follows duplicates a story in the Prose Edda where Thor fishes for and temporarily captures the Midgard serpent. After this fishing expedition Hymir sets Thor several challenges to prove his strength, from carrying a whale home that they caught while fishing to breaking a seemingly unbreakable crystal cup; the cup is only broken when a giantess tells Thor to break it against Hymir's head. Hymir then tells the two Gods to take the cauldron if they can carry it and while Tyr can't Thor does. They leave with the Cauldron only to have Hymir and his giants chase them, causing Thor to turn, set down the cauldron, and pull out Mjolnir. After killing all the giants the two head back to Aegir's hall with the cauldron[4].

In the Thrymskvida Thor's hammer is stolen by the giant Thrym who demands Freya as his bride. Freya refuses but Heimdall devises a plan to send Thor in Freya's place, dressed as a bride with his face concealed by a veil, accompanied by Loki similarly disguised as his handmaiden. The two travel this way to Thrym's home, where the giant is eager to claim Freya as his bride although he is puzzled by her strange appearance. He comments on her enormous appetite for food and drink, to which Loki replied it was due to the bride fasting for eight days. Thrym then goes to kiss the fake Freya only to exclaim at her terrifying eyes, to which Loki replies that the bride hasn't slept for eight days. At this point the giant calls for the hammer to be brought and placed in the bride's lap to sanctify the marriage. As soon as the hammer is back with Thor he sets about killing the giants surrounding them.

The Alvissmal tells the story of a confrontation between Thor and the dwarf, Alviss, who has decided to marry Thor's daughter. The dwarf appears suddenly and declares that he is taking Thor's daughter with him as his bride, saying she was promised to him; Thor disputes this because he was unaware of any match being made for Thrud. The two then engage in a battle of wits with Thor questioning Alviss about the name for specific things – including earth, sky, moon, and sun – among the men, Aesir, Vanir, giants, elves, and dwarves. So, for example, Thor asks what all beings call wood and Alviss responds:

> "Wood it's called by men, and mane of the valleys by the gods,
> Slope-seaweed by humankind,
> Fuel by the giants, lovely boughs by the elves,
> Wand the Vanir call it"
> (Larrington, 1996, page 113).

In this way the two go back and forth until Thor declares that while Alviss may have great knowledge Thor has tricked him because the sun is rising. At that point Alviss is turned to stone by the daylight, decidedly losing the contest, and Thor's daughter is spared having to marry him.

In the Thórsdrápa we learn of the events when Thor travels to the land of giants to confront a giant named Geirrod. There are differing accounts of this story because it was very popular, with some saying that Thjálfi was Thor's companion while the others that it was Loki. In either case Thor goes into the land of giants without his hammer. On the way to confront Geirrod, Thor encounters the giantess, Gríd, one of his father's mistresses, who advises him that Geirrod is a dangerous foe; to help him she gives him iron gauntlets, a belt of strength, and her staff. These prove invaluable as he continues on. First he needs to ford a river but as he tries to cross it the water floods, the levels raised by Geirrod's daughter, Gjalp, who is either urinating into it or adding her menstrual flow. Thor hurls a stone at her to stop the torrent and then wades to shore, clutching a rowan tree to help him. Thor and his companion continue on and arrive at a building, sometimes described as a goat shed, where Thor sits in a chair only to find the chair lifting beneath him and pressing him against the ceiling; both of Geirrod's daughters, Gjalp and Greip, are beneath it. Thor uses the staff Gríd gave him to push back against the ceiling forcing the chair down and killing the two giantesses. Thor finally arrives at Geirrod's house, where the giant hurls a red-hot iron rod at the God. Thor catches it with the iron gauntlets given him by Gríd and throws it back at Geirrod who has hidden behind a pillar. The rod goes through the pillar and kills the giant.

In the Sagas

References to Thor are not as abundant in the Sagas as they are in the Eddas but there are some appearances by the God himself, his statues, or mentions of his worship and so reading and studying the sagas is important. They also provide a necessary wider context for the period in which he was honoured and the culture that he comes from, particularly in Iceland.

Ynglinga Saga – Thor appears here in a heavily euhemerized form, depicted as a human priest of the god Odin. In this account Thor's mythological home of Thrudvangr is explained as a place in Sweden that was given to him by Odin (Hollander, 2007).

Njal's Saga – There is one account in Njal's Saga where a man named Killer-Hrapp sneaks into a temple owned by Earl Hakon and strips the statues of their gold, including one of Thor in a wagon. He moves them outside then burns the temple down. The earl's wife initially believes the God-statues were miraculously spared but her husband correctly guesses that a human hand must have moved them out, then says:

"The Gods are in no hurry to avenge themselves, but the man who did this will be banished from Valhalla [Odin's hall] and never enter there." (Cook, 2001).

There is also a particularly interesting conversation later in the saga between a heathen woman named Steinunn and a Christian named Thangbrand where the two debate theology. Steinunn claims that Thor had challenged Jesus to a fight but that the Christian saviour wouldn't dare fight the heathen god of thunder. Thangbrand replies that Thor would not exist if the Christian God didn't want him to. Steinunn replies to that with a poetic piece claiming that Thangbrand's previous shipwreck, and loss of his vessel, was Thor's direct action unmitigated by Thangbrand's God.

Egil's Saga – In Egil's Saga the eponymous protagonist calls on Thor, along with Odin, Freyr, and Njord, to curse the king who has ruined him, asking that Gods banish the king from the land. This is part of a larger effort by Egil to curse the king which at one point involves setting up a nithstang[5] to turn the land spirits against him.

Eyrbyggja Saga – this saga describes, in part, the journey of a man named Hrolf who was so deeply dedicated to Thor that he changed his name to Thorolf. He kept a temple to Thor in Norway and when he later moved to Iceland he brought the pillars of his temple with him, using them to find the place to land in his new home. One of these pillars featured an image of Thor and on reaching the shore of Iceland Thorolf threw them overboard asking Thor to show him where to land and build. Not only did Thorolf build his new house there but he also built a new temple to Thor; adjacent to this temple was a field which where Thorolf held assembly. This field was declared holy, meaning that no one could shed human blood as part of feuds or defile it with urination or defecation.

Thor in My Life

Thor features in so many myths and stories it's hard to choose one favourite but if I did have to choose one it would be the same as my favourite Odin story, the Hárbarðsljóð in the Poetic

Edda. Not only does this story give a lot of insight into who both of these deities are and their personalities but it is also in my opinion a fun story to read. The image of Odin in disguise bandying words and barbs with his son amuses me, and I love the dichotomy of Thor focusing on martial successes while Odin brags about more venal ones.

For people just getting into Heathenry I do, of course, recommend reading the myths and stories but that can be a confusing and convoluted venture, especially given the variety of translations available. There are two main books that I suggest starting with at the very beginning, especially if you have no real previous experience with or knowledge of Norse myths. D'Aulaires 'Book of Norse Myths' is written for children but can be a good starting point even for adults. The myths are retold in a very basic and straightforward way but it covers all the important details. The illustrations are fun and convey a good sense of each deity.

I'd also suggest Kevin Crossley-Holland's 'The Norse Myths'. It is a collection of modern retellings of the major myths but it does a very good job of capturing the essence of each tale as well as, in my opinion, the personality of each deity. It's a good way to get a feel for the myths before plunging into the various translations and often difficult text of the source material. I've found that its very helpful to have this basic sense of the stories first to provide context when reading the older myths so that when you find a more difficult bit you aren't totally adrift.

Both of these resources are good places to start for people of almost any age and most reading levels, although the Crossley-Holland book is of course a bit more advanced than D'Aulaires.

End Notes

1 It may seem odd to some readers to begin a book such as the Prose Edda which is about the Norse Gods by establishing not only that they are actually humans but also tying them to

characters from classical works like the Odyssey and Aeneid. This was not uncommon, however, for western European writers around the end of the first millennia and we see various myths being anchored in classical works or the Bible. This might be done to give more prestige to the stories of the culture in question at a time when classical literature was highly valued or might have been done to avoid criticism by the Christian church for recording pagan myths.

In any event while the relating of the myth may begin this way (we also see this with the Irish Lebor Gabala Erenn being anchored in Biblical myth) they generally very quickly move into telling the pagan stories without much external veneer. The idea of the deities as mere human characters, however epic or wonderous, is usually left behind by the stories themselves.

2 Ragnarok is the predicted doom or twilight of the Gods and represents the final confrontation between the Norse Gods and the forces of entropy and chaos that they have been fighting. Each deity faces off against an antithetical being, excepting only Heimdall who battles the hound that guards the gates of Helheim. This destruction is supposed to pave the way for a new beginning and a new world, populated by the next generation of Aesir. Given that we know when Baldur died he went to Helheim and so didn't cease to exist there is some room for supposition here about what exactly happens to the original Aesir.

3 In this particular story Tyr is said to be the son of the giant, Hymir, although his parentage is given differently elsewhere. Larrington suggests that Tyr was not the original companion to Thor in this poem but was substituted in later which may explain the discrepancy in his characterization in this piece. In her notes on the poem Larrington gives both Loki and Thjálfi as possible original alternates to Tyr.

4 This poem also includes a reference to Thor's goat being

lamed but attributes it to Loki rather than Thjálfi.

5 A Nithstang is a kind of curse pole, usually affixed with a severed horse's head, carved with runes, intended to so anger the land spirits or elves that they would flee an area. This would result in ill luck and disaster more generally.

Chapter 3

Thor in Other Places

Thor wasn't only an immensely popular deity in Iceland and in the main Norse cultures, but he is also found outside the Norse cultural world. Worship of Thor is seen in Germany and England, as well as in some of the Celtic countries that had Norse influence. In some cases, such as Germany and England, we find Thor under a different name which is linguistically and culturally related to the Norse Þorr, while in areas that were influenced by the Norse directly during the Viking period we may find Thor under his Norse or Anglicized name. In all cases his popularity as a deity of the common person remains and many of his associations and possessions are the same or very similar, for example his propensity for defending humanity against forces of entropy and his use of a hammer as a weapon.

There is always a debate about whether appearances of deities in related cultures are the same deity through different cultural lenses or are merely reflections of a similar concept. Which case is true is a matter of perspective and how a person views deity more generally. To some Thor is a unique deity who belongs to the Norse and the related Gods like Donar and Thunor would be considered cultural cousins and perhaps very closely related energies but still seen as individual beings in their own right. This would apply even to various beings all named Thor but existing in different specific cultures, so that some might even argue that Icelandic Thor and Norwegian Thor have become separate individuals after 1000 years of divergent development. In contrast other people see such deities which have emerged from the same ultimate cultural source as continuing to be the same singular deity even divided by time, distance, and different understandings and mythology. This is a complex and nuanced conversation with many possible shades of agreement or disagreement between the most extreme opposite views, which would be on the one hand seeing every single deity even within one singular culture as a unique manifested being while on the other hand the opposite extreme would be to see any and all Gods as the same divine power appearing in different guises. There is no right or wrong answer, only opinions, so in this chapter the information will be presented as it is and the reader may decide for themselves how closely they believe these beings are to Thor or how separated from him.

Thor in Germany

One of the main places that we find evidence of Thor outside the Norse is in Germany. The Germanic thunder God shared a clear root, agreed on by scholars, with the Norse Thor; in Germany Thor was known as Donar, and as elsewhere was most strongly connected to thunder.

Jacob Grimm[1] writes about Donar extensively in his 'Teutonic Mythology volume 1', comparing him to the Roman Jupiter and Dis Pater, as well as drawing on Norse sources for comparison. Grimm chose to emphasize Donar's fatherly aspects along with his thundering aspects. Quoting Grimm:

> *"And here I must lay stress on the fact, that the thundering god is conceived as emphatically a fatherly one, as Jupiter and Diespiter.... For it is in close connexion with this, that the mountains sacred to him also received in many parts such names as* Etzel [noble one, possibly related to 'little father'], Altvater [old father], Grossvater [grandfather]. *Thorr himself was likewise called* Atli, *i.e. grandfather."* (Grimm, 1888, page 169).

He discusses Donar's links to mountain names in detail, tying some of them to Roman names involving Jupiter and others to forms using names closer to the Norse Thor. In this way Grimm argues both for a connection between Donar and the fatherly aspects of Jupiter as well as tying him directly to the Norse Thor.

Thor is also compared to Hercules by Grimm and by Tacitus, writing about the Germanic tribes in the first century CE. Tacitus was writing using the Interpretatio Romana which was a system whereby Classical commentators would name the Gods of other cultures with the names of their own Gods so that their readers, Greek or Roman, would understand the deity being written about. This system is helpful in that it allows us now to draw conclusions about what features in a deity made the Romans identify them as a certain Roman God but is problematic because it reduces the nuances and ignores the differences between the deities being compared. Nonetheless, having Tacitus equate Donar to Hercules is useful here. It is likely that the comparison arose due to Donar's use of a hammer and Hercules' club as well as both being renowned for their strength. Tacitus also mentions at least one sacred grove dedicated to this Germanic 'Hercules' (Birley, 1999).

Like the Norse Thor, Donar is described as being bearded and having red hair, and it is said that when he is angry he blows through his red beard and causes thunder. He is also described as *"a tall, handsome, red bearded youth"* (Grimm, 1888, page 177). Grimm also mentions that sometimes people in distress would invoke Thor's beard. The physical appearance of Donar then would seem to be in line with the Norse descriptions. Grimm also emphasizes Donar's connections to wagons as another point he believes shows that Thor and Donar are either the same deity or close reflections of the same deity.

Thursday was sacred to Donar and still bears his name in German, Donnarstag. There was a prohibition against both carving and spinning on Thursday evenings, with being struck by lightning as a possible punishment for violating this (Grimm, 1888). Prior to Christianization Grimm suggests that Donar and Thursday may have held the same sacredness and esteem that would later be shifted to Sundays.

Donar was strongly associated with throwing stones down from the sky, which would embed themselves in the earth, but when found were thought to be charms against lightning. These stones had various folk names including: donnerstein [Donar's stone], donneräxte [Donar's axe], donnerhammer [Donar's hammer] (Grimm, 1888). These could be understood either as thunderstone, axe, and hammer or as Thor's stone, axe, and hammer respectively. These flint stones, usually prehistoric knives or axes, are also known as albschosse, or elfshot, indicating some crossover and dichotomy between the folklore of Donar in the storm and the more dangerous elves travelling out to attack humans.

The sign of the hammer was used for blessings and a hammer could be thrown to confirm the legal purchase of land (Grimm, 1888). This further indicates the association of the hammer with Donar, but hammers and thunderstones are not the only things connected to this deity. In southern Germany in the 19th century the stag beetle [Lucanus cervus] was called by the folk name 'donnergueg' [Donar's beetle]; the insect has folk associations with lightning and fire and is thought to live in oaks (Grimm, 1888). The houseleek is also worth mentioning, as a plant which is called 'donnerbart' [Donar's beard] and which is said to protect against lightning (Grimm, 1888). Karen Jolly also mentions the houseleek in her book 'Popular Religion in Late Saxon England' where she discusses its use in exorcizing dangerous spirits and cleansing.

There are many places named after Donar, usually with his name combined with words like 'way', 'mountain', and 'wood'. As with other locations that bear Thor's name elsewhere these indicate both his widespread popularity and specific things he is often associated with. However, in Germany there is a lack of personal names based on Donar, which is a clear difference from the Norse areas where Thor forms a compound with many names.

Grimm argues strongly that Donar would later be conflated with the Christian Devil. This is largely his conjecture but does fit a wider pattern of demonizing pagan popular pagan deities to discourage their worship. Grimm's main points rest on Donar's connection with goats and the Christian association between goats and the Devil as well as Donar's connection to fire and the colour red.

Thor in England

In England among the Anglo-Saxons Thor was called Thunor. Thunor's name is found in many place name compounds, especially in the territories held by the Saxons and the Jutes (Turville-Petre, 1964). As with the other cultural variations his name means 'thunder', and he was often compared or equated to Jove or Jupiter. Unfortunately the Anglo-Saxons converted to Christianity early and left us little material to work with; what we do know about him will be reviewed here.

Thunor was associated with thunder. The Old English word for thunder is 'ðunorrad' meaning 'Thunor's travelling' likely referencing the idea of Thunor passing through the sky during storms (Turville-Petre, 1964). This is in line with wider beliefs relating to Thor across Germanic cultures.

There is at least one preserved baptismal vow from around the 8th century CE in which the person explicitly renounces Thunor, Woden, and Saxnot (Turville-Petre, 1964). Thunor's primary placement in the list may indicate his importance overall in the pantheon; certainly it would seem to affirm his popularity. When a person was converting they would be expected to deny their previous Gods and the order that this denial occurred in is significant.

There's some supposition that Thunor may have wielded an axe. This is based on extrapolating out from an Old English reference which said that the devil was struck by the thunder with an axe (Turville-Petre, 1964).

Interestingly, during the later period when the culture had been Christianized, it was not Thunor that the Anglo-Saxon priests railed against but Thor (Turville-Petre, 1964). This indicates that the culture had thoroughly subsumed its own Heathen past but was dealing with the Norse Heathen influx during that period. As a result we do see a blend of both Thunor and Thor material in these areas.

Thor in Celtic Countries

Perhaps surprisingly we do find Thor in a variety of Celtic language speaking countries, brought there through Norse influence. In these cases we are not looking at a cognate of Thor that diverged from a singular Indo-European or proto-Norse root but rather at Thor as he is understood in Norse culture seen through the lens of the Celtic cultures

Scotland – Scotland was influenced by the Norse for roughly 700 years, between the 8th to mid-15th centuries CE, with the 9th through 11th centuries having the greatest cultural impact. This influence was the strongest in the outlying areas and islands[2] (Barrett, 2008).

McNeill in 'The Silver Bough' suggests that its possible the Heathen altars may have been kept next to the oratory of the Celtic Churches, around a central hearth area, during the uneasy conversion period[3]. She is clear that there is no direct evidence of this but posits the possibility given the shift from pagan to Christian in the Norse influences areas and the lingering Heathen beliefs. This would have reflected a similar concept, if not literal practice, as we see in Iceland where civil war over conversion was averted with an agreement to Christianise the country to satisfy evangelicals while still allowing Heathen practice in the home to appease those who did not want to convert.

We can also look at what we have for Yule traditions in Scotland for lingering evidence of Thor's presence. In Scotland

McNeill states that while Odin may be known as the Yule Father it is Thor to whom this holiday actually belongs, as does all of the month of December. A Yule log of oak was traditionally burnt and Thor was asked to bring a prosperous new year. She relates a story of Norsemen in Scotland celebrating Yule with a great feast and then a bonfire, around which they danced and then chant *"Thor with us, Thor and Odin! Haile Yule, haile!"* (McNeill, 1961, p. 52).

The Orkney Islands - These were originally a Celtic territory, however, prolonged Norse occupation shifted the culture in a different direction. Because of this we find Norse mythology and concepts in the Orkneys including the Wild Hunt, Odin, Trolls (under the name of trows), and Thor. One piece of evidence of Thor's presence in the Orkneys are the so-called thunderstones, pieces of quartz, flint, or similar crystals found in fields; these stones are believed to fall to earth during storms (Towrie, 2019). As might be expected, given their assumed origins, the thunderstones are believed to be hurled down to earth by Thor as he works to defend the human world. In folklore the projectiles are said to be aimed at trolls, thrown from above as Thor passed by to help keep the dangerous creatures in check. A thunderstone found on earth is a protective charm against these beings and might also be incorporated into the walls of a house to protect it from lighting (Towrie, 2019).

Ireland – Thor had a foothold in Ireland, particularly in Dublin where there was a strong Norse influence. The Norse in Ireland were commonly referred to as Muintir Tomhar [Thor's people] indicating his wide popularity there. There was a sacred grove outside the city called Coill Tomhair [Thor's wood]. This grove was important enough to merit Brian Boru going out of his way to have some of his men burn it when his army took Dublin from the Norse who had settled it (Colm, 2013).

In the 10th century there are accounts of a statue of Thor in Dublin which the Irish Christians spoke out against and whose shrine was raided by the Irish king, Maelseachlainn, in 994 CE; this raid also included the theft of an oath ring dedicated to Thor (Ellis Davidson, 1964).

Thor in My Life

My own practice of Heathenry began in 2006. Before that I had focused exclusively on Irish paganism but in late 2005 I began to study Asatru and Germanic paganism. At first my approach was to keep the two spiritualities entirely separate but as I studied more and saw the crossover between the cultures, especially in Celtic language speaking areas that had a lot of Norse influence I started to see them as less contradictory and more potentially complimentary. My approach was born out of the gradual realization that, firstly, the two cultures have a great deal in common, and secondly that there is historical precedent for the blending and melding of Norse and Celtic tradition. The two cultures did historically interact and influence each other; the Norse invaded and settled parts of Ireland and the Irish were in Iceland.

Much of what I studied involved looking at separate sources, a wide variety of both Celtic, Irish, and Norse material that only occasionally overlaps. The main sources that I use to understand how the cultures interacted and affected each other involve looking at Celtic areas with strong Norse influence that have been preserved, including the Orkney Islands and some Scottish material, such as McNeill's 'Silver Bough' series. Although my own focus is Irish, I find the Scottish and Orkney material easier to access and it provides a useful template to understand the pattern of cultural interaction. I have also found books like 'Lady with a Mead Cup', 'Beyond Celts, Germans, and Scythians', and 'In Search of the Indo-Europeans' helpful in understanding the ancient roots that the two cultures share.

I also focus on the Viking presence in Ireland. Viking influence in Ireland began around 800 CE and by 950 CE there were established Viking settlements in Dublin, Cork, Limerick, and Wexford (Viking Answer Lady, 2012). For most of this period the Viking invaders and settlers were still pagan, although the Irish at this point had converted to Christianity. There is significant archaeological evidence of the Norse presence in Ireland during this period, including burials (Fischer, 2012). Evidence also indicates that the Norse settlers assimilated to life in Ireland by adopting the lifestyles of the Irish (Preet, 2010). There is some evidence that surviving Irish customs surrounding midwinter are Norse in origin, the result of Irish assimilation of practices brought over by Norse settlers (Preet, 2010). Certainly such cultural "sharing" is seen in Scotland where the Norse also raided and settled, so it's reasonable to assume that the same would occur in Ireland. Similarly, Iceland shows Irish influences with many examples of Irish names and nicknames recorded; equally influential, many of the women taken in raids were Irish and were the mothers of later generations (Clements, 2005).

Since then I've shifted into a different direction, although one that's no less syncretic in approach. I focus less on the Gods, by any names, and more on the Hiddenfolk or Good Neighbours within these same cultures. But I still remember how important it was for me to stop seeing a rigid division between cultural groups and to understand that there was a lot of movement and interaction historically. This also allowed me to see Thor's place in locations outside traditionally Norse areas which helped me to understand the flexibility and movability of the Gods.

End Notes

1 Jacob Grimm is a useful source but also can be problematic and must be understood in the proper context. Grimm was writing late in the 19th century during a period when scholarship was not as rigorous as it is today. An author could write a great deal of supposition or tenuously supported theories without needing to use supporting texts or references and this is also

a time period where we see a great deal of folklore recorded by wealthy academics who were not directly part of the culture or subcultures they were recording; rather they wrote as outside observers and often retold rather than directly recorded. Grimm is a reasonably reliable source for the time period but it must be kept in mind that some of what he says is found no where else except in his writings.

2   This is especially true of Orkney but because Norse influence there was so profound that area will be addressed separately in a subsequent section.

3   To describe the conversion period among the Norse areas as uneasy is perhaps a bit too much of an understatement. While the Celtic language areas converted peacefully – so much so that the concept of white martyrdom was created to allow people to still have that goal even in areas without violence – the Norse areas were much more violent. McNeill retells an account of Olaf Tryggvason, the king of Norway, travelling to Orkney and threatening its ruler; Earl Sigurd was told he and his people could convert or Olaf would put them all to the sword. Sigurd initially refused, saying that he would not go against his ancestral beliefs, but when Olaf raised his sword to follow through with his threat Sigurd relented (McNeill, 1956).

Chapter 4

Thor's Possessions, Symbols and Associations

Although Thor's role in mythology can sometimes seem simple, with his straightforward defending of civilization against giants, Thor is a multifaceted God. This is shown by his many associations and symbols as well as the way that humans looked to him for almost everything in their lives one way or another. Thor influenced weather for good and ill, blessed a variety of human transitions from birth through death, and was a consecrator of oaths.

In this chapter we will look at each of his possessions, symbols, and associations one by one. These may appear in mythology or in later folk belief and taken together they give us a much clearer picture of how people across time have understood Thor and what they have looked to him for in their lives.

Home

Thor lives in Thrudheim (alternately Thrúðvangar) in a hall named Bilskirnir. Thrúðvangar means 'plains of power' according to Young, although Thruð may also be read as strength; Thrudheim could be read as 'strength home'. The Grímnismal describes the hall as being the largest of any of the Gods and claims it has six hundred and forty floors (Young, 1964). The text also describes Thrudheim this way:

> "A land is holy, which I see situated; Near the Aesir and elves; Still in Thrudheim shall Thor be; Until the powers are riven." (Lindow, 2001, page 292).

This tells us some helpful things about the location and nature of

Thor's home which are worth considering.

It's possible that some people who die go to Thor's hall in the afterlife, although beliefs about the afterlife among the Norse tend to be complex and sometimes contradictory. Thor's hall is mentioned as one possible destination in the afterlife for common people in a section of the Harbardsljod where Odin disguised as the ferryman, Hardbard, mocks Thor by saying while Odin gets the nobles who fall in battle Thor gets the common folk. This reflects the wider belief that Thor was a god of the common man and protector of humanity at large.

Mjolnir

Thor's most famous possession by far is his hammer, named Mjolnir. This hammer is of course not an ordinary possession but a special treasure; it was created by the dwarves Sindri (alternately Eitri) and Brokkr as part of a competition that Loki had dared them into to prove their skill with his own head as the forfeit if they won. Watching them work and realizing that the creation of Mjolnir would tip the balance in their favour Loki intervened, going in the shape of a fly and biting the dwarf pumping the bellows so that he faltered (Crossley-Holland, 1980). This is why Mjolnir's handle is short, because the forging wasn't perfect. Otherwise the hammer is a superb weapon which always returns to Thor's hand when thrown.

Thor uses Mjolnir to defend the Gods and the human world from dangerous beings including giants who would otherwise bring chaos and death. His fighting method is as straightforward as his weapon; he strikes directly at his enemies with his hammer or throws it.

Young interprets Mjolnir's name as meaning 'crusher' but the etymology is contested and there are multiple theories. Simek prefers to look to the older Proto-Norse roots then out to related cultures like Russian and Slavic where words which share the same root mean lightning and hence *"the one who makes lightning"*;

he also notes connections to Old Norse and Icelandic words for fresh snow and whiteness giving a meaning of *"shining lightning weapon"* (Simek, 1984, pages 219 – 220).

In the Thrymskvida Thor's Hammer is stolen and must be retrieved, demonstrating perhaps the importance of Mjolnir which can't be left in the hands of the giants. The hammer is used in that story to hallow the lap of the bride (actually Thor in disguise) and we also find images of the hammer on rune stones, indicating a potential consecratory nature to the weapon (Simek, 1993). In the Prose Edda there is a story about Thor returning his goats to life after eating them that specifies he used Mjolnir to consecrate the skins and bones as part of the process (Young, 1964). We see the Hammer used to bless brides, new-borns, and also during funerals, showing its versatility as an item of consecration; there is even a reference in one story to the practice of making a sign of Thor's Hammer over a drink before consuming it (Ellis Davidson, 1964). Thor's Hammer was also used as a religious symbol, cast as a pendant and worn by Heathens during the early Christian era to differentiate themselves from the new religion.

Thor's Hammer pendant

Related to the above entry we also have the Thor's Hammer pendant as a symbol of Thor. This is a very popular item today, worn by modern Heathens and Asatruar as symbols of their faith in the Norse Gods but it has roots in the pagan past. Examples of Thor's Hammer rings can be traced back to the 6th century in Anglo-Saxon England and the 8th century in northern Germany and Thor's Hammer pendants to a 9th century Viking burial in England (Ewing, 2008). The pendants would become popular in the 10th century during the conversion period when those who held belief in the Aesir would wear them to differentiate themselves from the Christians; evidence suggests that sometimes both crosses and Thor's Hammer pendants were cast in the same mould to keep up with the demand for the jewellery, with the smiths merely reversing the bail (Simek, 1993). Because of this some museum replica Hammers resemble upside down crosses.

Belt

In one story Thor was travelling without his famous hammer and stopped to visit the giantess, Gríd, who gave him three items to help him confront a dangerous giant and his daughters. These items included a belt which would enhance his strength; some accounts claim the belt doubled Thor's already impressive physical strength (Simek, 1993; Ellis Davidson, 1964). There is some debate about whether the belt that Thor possessed which doubled his strength was his own or was the one Gríd had given him (Turville-Petre, 1964).

Gloves

Like his belt these gloves were given to him by Gríd. In some accounts they are gauntlets made of iron and they magnify his strength. They also may have allowed him to lift his hammer (Ellis Davidson, 1964).

Staff

Called Grídarvolr, the staff features in a story where Thor must face a giant and his fearsome daughters without Mjolnir. To help him the giantess, Gríd, gives him a belt and gloves to enhance his strength as well as the staff Grídarvolr which allows him to overcome a flooded river and defeat the giant's daughters. The name means 'Grídr's wand' (Simek, 1993).

Goats

Thor travels in a chariot pulled by two goats named Tanngrisnir and Tanngnjostr, or 'Teeth-barer' and 'Teeth-grinder' (Simek, 1993). These two goats can be killed and eaten one night and will return to life whole and healthy the next day as long as their unbroken bones are wrapped in their skins overnight. In one story Thor is travelling and is accompanied by two children, Thjálfi and Röskva; despite being warned not to break any of the goats' bones during dinner Thjálfi does so to get at the marrow making the goat lame afterwards. As punishment the two are bound to Thor as his servants afterwards.

Thor's temples and shrines featured statues of him which sometimes were described as the God in a chariot pulled by the two goats, with the goats carefully carved and decorated (Turville-Petre, 1964). In some versions of the Thórsdrápa when Thor first arrives in Geirrod's land it says he went into a goat shed. Turville-Petre suggests that goats would have been Thor's sacred animal in the same way that the boar was sacred to Freyr and this seems logical given how often goats are associated with him or appear with him.

Thor is sometimes called the Lord of Goats or the Chariot God (Simek, 1993).

Oak

The oak is associated with Thor and may have been a tree sacred to him during the pagan period. There's a river island in Sweden named Torsholma [Thor's Island] which may have held a sanctuary and there are several accounts of sacred places that held enormous oak trees dedicated to what Roman and Greek writers called a 'thunder god' (Ewing, 2008). Ellis Davidson in 'Gods and Myths of Northern Europe' affirms Thor's connection to the oak, and also the oaks' wider sacredness, mentioning that holy oaks might sometimes have sacred wells close by. More generally oaks are often associated with thunder deities in Indo-European cultures, probably because of the frequency of lightning strikes on them.

Rowan

The rowan is also associated with Thor. In the Thórsdrápa it's said that a rowan helped Thor get out of a flooded river and there is a proverb that says "*The rowan is the salvation of Thor*" (Turville-Petre, 1964, page 81). In a wider sense rowan is associated with protection from a variety of dangers including supernatural ones. Although this connection may not be as strong as Thor's connection to the oak it is an important one.

Protector of Humans

'Protector of humankind' is a name for Thor in the Hymiskvida and this particular association may have been part of his popularity or may reflect it. While other Gods tended to be more specific in their focus, such as Odin who was a patron of the nobility and poets, Thor was the God of the common person. As Ellis Davidson says in her book 'Gods and Myths of Northern Europe':

"*...he was the god supreme not only over the stormy sky, but also over the life of the community in all its aspects.*" (Ellis Davidson, 1964, page 75).

Thor was seen as guardian of people and the human world and one who could be prayed to and called on for this purpose.

Oath Ring

There are several references to oath rings dedicated to Thor being kept in his temples. These rings are not the kind worn on fingers but would be large enough to fit around the arm and, according to the Eyrbyggja Saga, weighed around 20 ounces (Magoun, 1949). Oath taking was a highly ritualized and extremely serious affair which involved not only holding the oath ring but also swearing on certain Gods possibly including Thor. Ellis Davidson supports Thor having this role in the 9th and 10th centuries, mentioning an oath given in the sagas which calls on Freyr, Njord, and Thor, but suggests that Thor hallowing oaths would have been a power he had taken over from Tyr[1].

Thunder

Thunder is associated with the passing of his chariot and with the sound of his hammer striking targets. 19th century folklore claims that the sound of thunder frightens away giants and trolls because it reminds them of Thor and his battle prowess (Thorpe, 1851). In the Orkneys until nearly the 20th century thunderstorms were called 'Guid's Withir' [God's weather] with the god in question being Thor (Towrie, 2019). Jacob Grimm in 'Teutonic Mythology' says that in Gothland thunder is called Thorsåken [Thor's driving] reinforcing the idea that it his wagon which causes the sound of thunder.

Weather

Thor is sometimes connected to weather, both good and bad. Just as he is a God of thunder he was also considered to be a storm God and events such as shipwrecks are sometimes attributed to Thor, as we see in Njal's Saga when a Heathen woman claims a particularly vocal Christian lost his ship at sea due to a storm Thor sent, comparing the severe weather to Thor's own assault. Ellis Davidson describes Thor as a God with *"...special dominion over the realm of the sky and over storms..."* (Ellis Davidson, 1964, page78). Ellis Davidson also says that Thor sent both rain and good weather to the human world. This is supported by Adam of Bremen who said about Thor that:

"They say he rules the air which controls the thunder and lightning, the winds and showers, the fair weather and the fruits of the earth" (Ellis Davidson, 1964, page 84).

Fertility

Thor is associated with fertility of both the land and of humans. His hammer was used in wedding ceremonies to hallow the bride and to bless the couple with fertility. He was also prayed to for the good weather which was essential for crops to grow (Grimm, 1888). Ellis Davidson explains it this way:

> "The cult of Thor was linked up with men's habitation and possessions, and with well-being of the family and community. This included the fruitfulness of the fields, and Thor, although pictured primarily as a storm god in the myths, was also concerned with the fertility and preservation of the seasonal round." (Ellis Davidson, 1975, page 72).

Ellis Davidson also connected Thor's marriage to Sif as one aspect of his relation to the fertility of the earth, seeing their marriage as symbolic of the union between sky/rain and earth/crops.

Funerals

Just as Thor blessed brides and brought fertility he also hallowed funeral rites. Images of Mjolnir have been found on cremation urns, evidence of Thor's connection to funerary practices, and Thor's Hammers have also been found in at least 40 burials (Simek, 1993). In the story of Baldur's funeral Thor is the one who blesses the funeral pyre with his hammer, indicating both that funeral fires would be blessed and that this was one of Thor's functions. The exact nature of this blessing was is unknown but in relation to Baldur specifically it could have been either a restorative act or one meant to protect him on his journey into Helheim, the realm of the ancestral dead (Turville-Petre, 1964). We might extrapolate outwards and imagine that this purpose held true for Thor's role in blessing funerals more generally.

Blessing

Although not as often acknowledged or appreciated today Thor was clearly a God associated with blessings. We have already mentioned Thor being invoked to bless brides, fertility, and funerals but his function as a deity of consecration goes further than that. There are accounts of Heathens carrying fire around their land while calling on Thor to bless the space as well as Heathens making the sign of the Thor's Hammer over their drinks before drinking (Simek, 1993; Turville-Petre, 1964). While it is uncertain whether making the sign of the Hammer over drinks was an older practice or one that developed in response to the Christian habit of signing the cross over food and drink to bless it the practice is well established during the conversion period and was no doubt significant to those who did it. There is also a 19th century Swiss folk practice of drawing a 'T' reminiscent of a Thor's Hammer over doorways to protect homes from storms and other dangers (Heyl, 1897). This may indicate a continuation of the use of this symbol for blessing and protection even into the early modern era.

Sea-faring

Thor is also a God who people would pray to for safety on the ocean and successful sea voyages. To some degree this related to his power to control storms, and therefore to send or restrain them, but there also seemed to be a wider concept of Thor protecting those who were abroad and guiding seafarers. For example, Helgi the Lean was known to pray to Thor for guidance and direction at sea; like many others when his ship approached Iceland to settle there he asked Thor to help him find the best place and then went where he felt he was being led (Turville-Petre, 1993).

Thursday

The fifth day of the week is named for Thor in several languages including Old English [Þuresdæg] English [Thursday], Dutch [Dondertag], Danish [Torsdag], and German [Donnarstag] all of which mean Thor's Day. This appears to have been a sacred day for Thor historically as even in the 7th century the bishop of Noyon had to speak to his congregation who were still keeping Thor's day holy (Ellis Davidson, 1964). Jacob Grimm also mentions prohibitions against spinning and carving on Thursdays which he relates to the cult of Donar [Thor] in his book 'Teutonic Mythology'.

Lindow suggests that the name for the day comes from the Interpretatio Germanica, where the Germanic tribes adapted the Roman names for the days of the week to their own use. In this system Dies Jovis, the fifth day named for Jupiter, was shifted to Thor's Day. Jupiter's use of lightning and association with thunder is a likely explanation for why Thor was syncretized to him and this day (Lindow, 2001). If this supposition is true then it's possible that the practices honouring Thor on this day developed later based on the idea that the day was sacred to him because of its name.

Thurisaz

Although this rune in the rune poems is most strongly associated with the dangerous giants there are some modern Heathens who have come to see it as Thor's rune. In this case they see it as a symbol of his protection against forces of entropy rather than a symbol of entropy itself.

In the Anglo-Saxon poem it is compared to thorns in a briar patch which cut those who touch it and cruelly entangles those who stumble into it.

"The thorn is exceedingly sharp,
an evil thing for any knight to touch,
uncommonly harsh on all who sit among them."

In the Norwegian and Icelandic it is compared to a certain

type of evil giant, bad luck, and illness or suffering of women.
Norwegian: *"Giant causes anguish to women;*
Ill-luck makes few men cheerful."
And the Icelandic: *"Giant*
suffering of women
and cliff-dweller
and husband of a giantess"

Thurisaz certainly has these energies within it, and is strongly masculine and aggressive, causing destruction, chaos, conflict and complications. It is the tangling brambles which ensnare and cause delay in our lives as well as complicating our plans, however all things have two sides - the briars which tangle and trap the fox offer shelter and protection to the mouse hiding within them. This aspect of Thurisaz is an ideal protection for the helpless, a powerful defence for the weak. Like the briar it is a neutral natural force which can cause harm or help depending on how we choose to interact with it. In modern times it is often associated with the god, Thor, defender of mankind, although it also symbolizes the enemies he fights. It represents power, strength, natural forces, male potency, aggression, conflict, protection, defence, and entanglement.

Thor in My Life

The story of Thor causing thunder is one that we tell often in my family. My children all went through phases where they were afraid of storms and to help them each get over that fear we would sit and watch the rain. When the lightning would flash and the thunder would sound I would talk to them about Thor, who he was and how he would battle against the dangerous giants. I would tell them that the lightning was the flash of his hammer flying in the sky and the thunder was the sound of Thor's chariot rolling through the clouds.

Of course, these are fanciful explanations and we would also talk about the scientific causes behind the phenomena. But I've never seen science and spirituality as conflicting and I have raised my children to believe that both options can be simultaneously possible, that we can understand the atmospheric conditions that create lightning and the accompanying sound of thunder and also find comfort in the stories of Thor travelling through the sky in his goat-drawn chariot to protect our world. Sometimes even knowing the real world cause its nice to have another layer of belief that goes along with that.

I find it comforting even as an adult to believe that Thor still watches over the human world, that he is still guarding us against dangers. The image of him casting stones down at trolls as he patrols the skies is a deeply reassuring one in a world that can sometimes feel uncertain and threatening. Whether we are talking about literal threats or figurative ones, our world is not always a safe place and the idea that there is a deity who watches over that world is one I like.

End Notes

1 There are several authors who feel that Tyr was probably the original pre-eminent deity of the Norse pantheon, but that over time his power was diminished as the cult of Odin came into prominence and Odin took over many of Tyr's functions as head of the pantheon. It is possible that some of that power was also shifted to Thor, such as the hallowing of oaths, and Ellis Davidson provides good evidence both of Thor's role in the ritual of oathing as well as the presence of sacred oath rings dedicated to Thor.

Chapter 5

Thor in the Modern World

As beloved as Thor was during the pagan period he is also certainly well loved during the modern era. For some people this appeal is rooted in his historic image while for others their love of Thor has grown from encounters with him in modern media. In this chapter we will look at Thor's appearances across multimedia, from comics to fiction to television and movies. Each of these is an aspect of Thor's modern mythology and while they may vary quite a bit from the older myths they do aggregate to create who Thor is today.

We'll look at each category of Thor's modern appearances as a separate section, and discuss the history and context of them in as much detail as possible for this text. Of course within a Pagan Portal we are limited in exactly how in-depth we can get so I recommend Martin Arnold's book 'Thor: Myth to Marvel' if you would like a really deep dive into this subject.

Opera

In Wagner's Das Rheingold, Thor appears under the name Donner. In this version he is not Odin's son but his brother-in-law and his main characterization is as a quick tempered, angry man wielding his hammer more than his mind. For the bulk of the opera Donner adds little to the storyline, which is about the theft of the ring from the Rhine maidens and the giants demand for Freya. Only at the end, when the problems have been solved by Loki and Odin, does Thor have a helpful showing when he uses a storm to clear the skies and create a rainbow bridge for the Gods.

Arnold in his book 'Thor: Myth to Marvel' dissects this appearance of Thor, along with many others, and specifically frames it within the cultural context of 19th century German nationalism. Wagner's Donner is embedded in a work that is culturally significant and parallels Jacob Grimm's conceptualization of the warrior-hero Donar.

Comic Books

Many people's modern understanding of Thor has been heavily influenced by the pop-culture of the 20th century, especially comic books. The Thor of the comic books, however, is often very different from the Thor of folklore and mythology and while the comics have acted as a good introduction for many people to Norse mythology they must not ever be taken as mythology in their own right; they were created purely for entertainment not religion.

DC – Thor appeared briefly as a character for DC in 1957, penned by Jack Kirby. This Thor was a template for the later Marvel Thor which was co-created by Kirby and has some similarities to the later comic incarnation.

Marvel Comics – Marvel introduced a character named Thor Odinson in 1962, the creation of writers Stan Lee, Larry Lieber, and Jack Kirby. This Thor was loosely based on the mythic deity, including his weapon being Mjolnir, but many liberties were taken in his characterization and backstory. Although in the early storyline Thor is described as a God later stories would shift this; rather than being a God, Marvel's Thor is from another world, a planet called Asgard where Thor's father, Odin, rules. Marvel also made Loki Thor's adopted brother and his mother the goddess Gaea, a noted departure from actual mythology and drew him as a beardless blond instead of a bearded red head.

The initial storyline for the character had him sent to earth by Odin without his memories as the human Donald Blake, a medical student. Blake eventually stumbles across Mjolnir in disguise and transforms into Thor, but at first the two act as alter egos for each other. Blake remains a doctor with nurse

Jane Foster helping him in his clinic, while Thor fights crime; eventually Thor chooses to stay on earth voluntarily to defend it against danger including the schemes of his brother Loki.

Over the decades multiple writers have handled Thor's comics resulting in many different ideas and storylines for the character. Thor was a founding member of the Avengers superhero group and appears in many of those comics as well as his own. In 2014 Thor was re-envisioned as a female character, although this new Thor was later revealed to be Thor's human girlfriend Jane Foster who was now wielding Mjolnir in the original Thor's stead when he was no longer able to do so. The original Thor, under the name Odinson, was brought back in 2016 in a darker comic series.

The popularity and influence of Marvel's Thor shouldn't be underestimated. 'The Mighty Thor' has seen more printings since its release than the Eddas have (Arnold, 2011). This, at the least, implies that Western audiences are far more familiar with comic book Thor than mythological Thor and that Marvel's creation is a cornerstone of Thor's contemporary mythology.

Brat-halla – Initially a web comic in the early 2000's and later collected and put out in a print edition, Brat-halla is the work of Jeffrey Stevenson, Seth Damoose, and Anthony Lee. The premise of the series is an envisioning of the Gods of Asgard, including Thor, as children parented by the adult Odin and Frigga. Some aspects stay true to mythology, such as Thor's strength, but obviously the plot lines themselves necessitate a lot of creativity and varying from known lore.

Modern Fiction

Magnus Chase and the Gods of Asgard – A young adult series by Rick Riordan, Thor features in four books including one which retells the story of his hammer being stolen, but with Thor removed as the main protagonist and the children of the series put in. He is described in a less than flattering way as something of a quick tempered jock, not terribly smart, who likes watching television and lacks personal hygiene.

Runemarks and Runelight – These are young adult novels by Joanne Harris which imagine an apocalyptic future after Ragnarok in which the Norse Gods have largely lost power and a new dangerous religion has risen. Thor doesn't appear directly but the main protagonist and the antagonist of the second book are directly and vitally connected to him.

American Gods - Thor appears in Neil Gaiman's 'American Gods', both the novel and the television series, but only very briefly. In the novel he is mentioned as Thor, son of Odin, who is a main character of the book under the name 'Mr. Wednesday', and the reader is told he killed himself in 1932. In the television show he appears in the second season episode 'Donar the Great' where the viewer learns Donar aka Thor was preforming as a strongman at a theatre run by his father in the 1930's; as in the novel the character commits suicide although in the show this happens in 1942.

Movies

The Thor of Marvel Comics appeared in a series of movies in the 21st century: Thor (2011), The Avengers (2012), Thor: The Dark World (2013), Avengers; Age of Ultron (2015), Thor: Ragnarok (2017), Avengers: Infinity War (2018), and Avengers: Endgame (2019). The first movie can stand alone, simply telling of Thor's quest to find his lost hammer and earn the right to wield it as he strives to defend the earth. The later movies are largely inter-related to each other and tell a more complex unfolding story both of Thor's relationship with Loki as well as his membership in the Avengers, a group of earth-based super heroes. In each film Thor is played by Chris Hemsworth and the actor's image has, for some people, become synonymous with Thor.

Television

The Almighty Johnsons - An Australian television show which aired between 2011 and 2013. It was based on the premise that the Norse Gods had reincarnated into human forms and the reincarnated Odin needed to find Frigga in order to restore the Gods to Asgard and full control of their powers. Thor in the series is living as a human named Derrick who is a goat farmer. Derrick is initially unaware of his divine nature until a chance meeting first with Tyr then with Odin. His personality on the show is similar to the Thor of the Eddas and popular understanding: fiery tempered, stubborn, and loyal. The character on the show also has some notable flaws unique to this fictitious depiction including homophobia. As with some other modern depictions this Thor is shown as less intelligent and brash to the point of dangerous to those who aren't truly his enemies.

Hercules the Legendary Journeys – Thor is in this usually Greek-centred show during a two episode story arc where the eponymous series hero travels to Asgard. The Thor shown in this show, while visually unfortunate, is fairly similar to the mythological Thor except for losing a fight against Hercules which seems unlikely.

Cartoons – The Marvel comic book character appeared in a variety of cartoons beginning with a 13 episode story arc in The Marvel Superheroes in the 1960's. In the 1980's he made short appearances on two Spiderman shows. In the 1990's Thor also had brief appearances in the animated shows the Fantastic Four and X-Men. In the 2000's he was a major character in the series The Super Hero Squad Show, and later in The Avengers Earth's Mightiest Heroes and Avengers Assemble. He had a small appearance in the 2013 Phineas and Ferb; Mission Marvel, and has also featured in several animated Lego movies with super hero themes.

Marvel Agents of S.H.I.E.L.D. – The Marvel movie version of Thor appeared in two episodes of the spinoff television series based on the cinematic world. The actor who has portrayed Thor in the movies, Chris Hemsworth, did not film the television show, rather pre-filmed footage was used.

The Incredible Hulk Returns – This 1988 made-for-TV movie features Thor as an ambivalent character complicating the life of Dr. Bruce Banner. Following earlier comic book canon, in this movie Thor has been banished from Asgard by Odin and his spirit trapped in his own hammer; when Mjolnir is found by a human Thor has no choice but to serve him, albeit unwillingly. Initially Thor appears as a disruptive force but over the course of the movie he shifts into a more heroic, or at least helpful, attitude.

Video Games

Marvel – Thor, unsurprisingly, is a character in several Marvel video games both as a background character and a playable one. These playable appearances include: Marvel Ultimate Alliance I and II, Marvel Superhero Squad, Thor: God of Thunder, Marvel Heroes, Marvel Future Fight, and Marvel Avengers Academy. This popularity reflects his wider popularity as a character in the franchise.

God of War – In this 2018 video game Thor is mentioned during the gameplay as a ruthless god who supports Odin's quest for knowledge by killing not only giants but anyone else necessary. His two sons have a larger role in the game and one of the goals of the player is to kill them.

Thor's journey across modern media has been a convoluted one; detached from mythology for the most part and used instead as a tool to either relay a socio-political message or as a vehicle of pure entertainment. The primary God of the Heathen Norse becomes, instead, a side character defined by his temper, an outcast who must earn his place back, or even the antagonist. Arnold may sum it up best:

"...ideas about Thor...have generally involved a shift away from the purview of scholars, polemicists, and the literati...and into mass markets, where entertainment substitutes for aesthetics and unbridled imagination substitutes for serious analysis and accuracy." (Arnold, 2011, page 159).

Despite this these modern depictions of Thor form a vital part of his mythology and do influence how people today understand and relate to the Thunder God.

Thor in My Life

I know that for some people who have come to Heathenry in the last decade the Marvel Thor movie was what first got them interested in the spirituality. I must admit that I didn't initially like the movie character of Thor, who I first saw in The Avengers movie. I can't say exactly why; just that I didn't enjoy Thor's portrayal in the film or the way Loki seemed more outright evil than nuanced the way he is in the mythology. Perhaps that's a pitfall of enjoying reading the mythology so much, I have a deeper investment in the stories as they were written than in the modern fictional re-tellings, even in comic or cinema form.

I hadn't seen the previous Thor movie because generally speaking super hero movies aren't my usual genre. Later though I did give the Thor movie a chance and, while the beginning didn't change my feelings from The Avengers, as the movie went on I found that I did like it better and better. I started to see why people might watch it and be drawn to Norse paganism or spirituality from there.

It is important to remember that the Thor of Marvel is a unique creation. There are aspects of the comic book and movie hero that are similar to the Thor of Norse myth but they also differ in important ways. And not only the space alien aspect. While Loki did often travel as Thor's companion he wasn't Thor's brother although modern understandings of him have been so heavily influenced by the movies in the last decade that many people now believe this.

Marvel's Thor isn't the Thor of Norse mythology but he is a captivating and intriguing character, and one who has a modern mythology around him.

Chapter 6

Connecting to Thor Today

In this chapter we will look at a variety of different methods and ideas that you can try if you'd like to build this connection for yourself. There isn't necessarily a right or wrong way to connect to a deity and what works for one person may not work for another. Also different faith traditions will have their own approaches and ideas for how one should connect to deities so some of the things presented here may or may not fit into specific approaches. This is meant to offer a broad overview that can then be tailored to fit the individual which should be kept in mind. If a certain concept speaks to you then try it, if one doesn't then skip it.

A Note about Racism in Modern Heathenry

It's unfortunately necessary, even in this day and age, to say this before we delve into the subject of Thor in the Modern world. While there are many, many good Heathens and Asatruar in the world who are genuinely honouring the Norse Gods there are also some people who have co-opted those Gods and the symbols connected to the culture for racist agendas and who call themselves Heathens. This has been an issue for a long time but over the last few years has become more prominent[1], and it is not something that can be ignored. Racism and White Nationalism can be very subtle, using what are termed 'dog whistles[2]' which are almost like a code that people within the movements recognize but that those outside may not; one example of this might be an emphasis in an article on ethnic preservation another more blatant one would be the use of the neo-Nazi 14/88.

This means that one must be careful and discerning when navigating the waters of modern Heathen material, and be very aware of the potential for subtle and less than subtle racist subtext. There are books out there with these agendas written into them and whose authors are advocates of White Supremacy. There are groups that are blatantly or subtly aligned with these agendas. All of which may not be obvious initially but must be watched out for by those who do not agree that skin colour impacts who the Gods can and do call.

When the mythology is studied I believe there is nothing in it that supports racist ideologies, and certainly looking at the historic culture doesn't. The Norse were travellers and settlers and there are things we can fairly criticize about them but they never seemed reluctant to mingle with other peoples or to mix their genetics. What made anyone part of the culture was being in the culture, the language and beliefs, not their skin colour.

I am part of a Heathen kindred which includes people of non-European ancestry and I would far, far rather stand in solidarity and worship with my Kindred sister, who is one of the best, most honourable people I know - and a devoted Thor's woman - than I would ever want to claim any kinship to some stranger who shares nothing with me but an illusory relation based on coincidental melanin similarity. My Kindred sister is part of my innangard, and her ancestry or ethnicity is a complete non-issue. And I am lucky to have her in my life and in my Kindred. Those who judge her as less or say she has no place in her religion do nothing but show their own lack of value in doing so. My own ancestry doesn't make me a better or worse Heathen, and the idea that it does shows a lack of knowledge of historic Heathenry in my opinion.

That all said let's move on into how to connect to Thor in the modern world.

Statues

One very simple way to begin connecting to Thor is to get a statue of him. We know from archaeology and historic accounts that there was a practice of carrying small statues of divinities, including Thor, on a person as well as larger more elaborate statues placed at ritual sites (Ewing, 2008). The small personal statues seem to have served as a kind of amulet although we may speculate that they may also have been used for small travelling shrines or worship.

One description of a large temple in Mæra, Norway, included a mention of a central, elaborately decorated statue of Thor seated in a wooden chariot pulled by two wooden goats carved in great detail (Ewing, 2008). An account of a statue of Thor at Hundorp, Norway, is similarly grand in its depiction and mentions that the statue held a hammer and was positioned on a platform which it could also be placed on when outside (Ewing, 2008). This is particularly interesting in that it shows that the statues could be moved indoors or outdoors as the occasion required and possibly also to move the statue out of inclement weather that might damage it. These shrine statues were very large, said to be life sized or perhaps larger than life.

When selecting a statue for yourself you should consider two factors in my opinion: what statue is going to work with your space and what statue appeals to you aesthetically. As with so many other things here there isn't any right or wrong answer but since the statue is supposed to be a tool to help you connect to the deity you want one that makes you think of Thor. Bigger isn't necessarily better and neither is any specific material, although an argument can be made for natural materials when possible.

There are many good statues of Thor on the market now; my personal favourite is a seated image by Paul Borda of Dryad Design. There are also museum replicas if you prefer something that has an older feel to it, or you can even fashion your own using any material you are comfortable working with. If you aren't comfortable making your own and can't find anything for sale that you like your other option would be to find someone who takes commission work willing to custom make one for you.

Altars and Shrines

Another good way to begin connecting to any deity is by setting aside a place in or around your home for them. This doesn't need to be anything fancy although you can certainly make it as complex or decorative as you like. The idea is to have something that makes you personally feel closer to the deity so whatever works for that purpose is good. Again this practice is something that we find references to in the written material, with sources talking about shrines to Thor in large public temples, groves, private homes, and even carried on individuals in the form of small statues (Ewing, 2008).

To set up an altar to Thor you could use a statue or picture that reminds you of him. As mentioned above there are many good options out there for statues in a variety of sizes and materials. If you don't like the idea of a statue you could use a picture, either artwork depicting Thor or any other image that reminds you of him, like a thunderstorm or even stylized Thor's Hammer. One description of a temple of Thor found in the Sturlaugs Saga Starfsama mentions golden game pieces, possibly from a Norse game called Hnefatafl (Lindow, 2001). This being the case you might even consider placing pieces or a small set of an appropriate strategy game on the altar or shrine.

Other items kept on the shrine or altar will depend a lot on you and your personal faith tradition but at the most basic an offering bowl or plate is necessary. I might also suggest considering an oath ring or replica Thor's Hammer as both were found or referenced in historic temples of Thor and could have use today either symbolically or for blessing. Again there's no requirement or standard for either item although the oath ring historically was said to be an arm-ring so you would want something bigger than a finger ring.

If you decide on an indoor space the first decision is whether it will be temporary or permanent. A temporary space can be set up and taken down again as needed while a permanent space would, of course, be there whenever its needed. The actual amount of space you need depends entirely on you and how big you want to make the shrine or altar. You can make use of a very small space with just a statue, candle, and bowl with everything sized to fit the area; I've seen museum replica Thor statues small enough to fit on a keychain that can be used for this purpose. You can also be as subtle as you like – there's no rule saying an altar or shrine has to loudly advertise what it is if you live in a religiously diverse household or just prefer not to draw attention to it. It's your spiritual area it should make you feel comfortable. That all said you can also go as big and elaborate with it as you like if that's what you want to do.

For an outdoor shrine or altar you want to find a space that is reasonably private and secluded. Beyond that, much like an indoor shrine, you can tailor the space to what suits you and make it as simple or detailed as you would like. I have seen outdoor shrines that are heavily decorated and complex and those that are nothing but a place for offerings next to a tree. The most important thing to remember in creating an outdoor space is that it will have to be able to hold up to whatever weather you get throughout the year, and you will need to be able to maintain it appropriately. If you want to have a statue outdoors you might want to find a stone statue or a resin image that's designed for outdoor use, carve something from wood[3], or use a natural object to represent Thor. One of the most beautiful outdoor shrine spaces to Thor that I have personally seen is at Brushwood in New York and featured a carved image that was out in a small clearing along with several other Norse deities; my own outdoor home shrine is a stone offering space in front of a large tree where the tree for me represents the World Tree.

Offerings

There is at least one reference in a saga to Thor being offered bread and meat[4] (Ewing, 2008). Grimm also references an offering to the Estonian Thunder God, who he connects to Thor, which involved an ox; this was done in the course of a prayer for good weather and bountiful crops (Grimm, 1888). There has been some supposition that goat might have been an appropriate offering as well because goats were a sacred animal to Thor. Historically it was also a known practice for feasts to be prepared and a portion to be offered to the Gods. Based on this you might decide to offer bread, meat, or to share portions of your own meals.

Modern heathens are eclectic in what they choose to offer the Gods but many feel that Thor accepts ale and beer. He does have a connection to beer as the one who journeyed to obtain the cauldron needed to brew ale for the Gods (Lindow, 2001). Personal taste may influence your choice of what to offer but dark ale and heavier beers are popular choices.

Guided Meditation to Thor

Another good way to begin to get to know a deity if you are more esoteric minded is with guided meditations or journeywork. For that reason I am including a simple guided meditation here for people to connect further to Thor. This approach is not to everyone's taste and if you personally do not utilize guided meditation in your spirituality you may of course skip ahead to the next section. Otherwise you may find this helpful in your attempt to get to know Thor better.

Experiences and interactions during this should be treated as if they are as real as anything in the waking world and I encourage people to journal their experiences immediately afterwards. Be careful what you say or agree to as oaths carry as much weight in meditations as if in ritual.

Sit comfortably somewhere that you won't be disturbed. Close your eyes. Take several slow, deep breaths. In your mind count down slowly from ten as you imagine yourself surrounded by white light.

See yourself walking down a sunlit path through the woods.

You are surrounded by oak trees, their boughs full of dark green leaves. The sun shines down filtering through the leaves onto the dirt path you are walking on. As you walk the trees around you begin to thin and you step out into a clearing in the woods. The woods around you are full of bird song but the clearing is still and waiting.

After a moment Thor emerges from the far side. Take some time to study him as he walks out of the trees. What is he wearing? How does he look to you? How does the energy around him feel? He approaches you and greets you, telling you who he is and welcoming you to this place. If you have any questions for him now is the time to ask, otherwise you can simply listen to whatever he has to say to you. He may have personal messages or insights for you or he may have more general things to say. Take as long as you need for this conversation, but be sure to thank him when you feel you are finished.

When Thor leaves turn and go back down the path. Go back through the tunnel of trees. The trees around you grow denser and fuller as you walk deeper into the forest. The light dims.

Take several slow, deep breathes. Feel your spirit settling fully back into your body. Wiggle your toes and fingers. Stretch slowly.

Open your eyes when you are ready.

You can repeat this meditation as often as you'd like, although you may find that Thor doesn't appear every time.

Sacred Sites

There are several real-world places that are associated with Thor or with the Aesir more generally and you might choose to visit these places, if you can, or to have pictures of them around you. These might include:

Upsala Sweden – the location of a well-known temple to Thor (and Frey and Odin)

Thorsberg Moor Germany – a site that contains votive deposits from the first to the fourth centuries CE

Thingvellir, Iceland – the place where the Allthing was held

Goðafoss – the place were its said that one of the leaders of Iceland threw his Godpillars into the waters after the country converted to Christianity. Legend says the posts are still there.

Prayers and Poetry

There are some historic prayers and hymns to Thor that have survived, occasionally in small sections, from the Germanic world and Iceland (Ewing, 2008). There are also many modern prayers written by contemporary devotees. Part of what connecting to Thor today involves is praying to him and appreciating poetry to him. For that reason in the chapter I'm going to include a selection of prayers and poems that a person might find helpful or inspiring, although I encourage you to write your own as well. You don't need pre-written prayers at all if you find they don't speak to you, so feel free to just speak from the heart if that's more comfortable.

Prayer to Thor
Thor be with me
This day and every day
As I go forth and as I return
Your hammer guard me

Invocation of Thor
We call to you defender of mankind
Chariot God, Earth's Son
Join us now as we gather to honour you
Be with us as we speak your name
Accept this offering
That we make in your name

For your blessing and protection
Thor, slayer of giants
Be with us

Prayer to Thor
Asa-Thor, mighty God
I call you today
As we seek to honour you
Ving-Thor, saining God
May you bless us
As we seek to honour you
Reidar-Thor, traveller of earth
May you guard us
As we seek to honour you
Thor, be with us
Now and always

Prayer for Travel
Asa-Thor, travelling God
May my way be clear before me
Donar, God of might and main
May your hammer ward my way
Thor, great God and protector of mankind,
May I travel timely along my way
Safely I go forth,
Safely I shall return
By my will, it is so

Children's Prayers

The following prayers are pieces I worked up for my own
children when they were small. They are meant to cover several
different aspects of life that children might feel like using prayer
for and to be fairly simple.

Prayer during Storms
Thunder, thunder
In the sky
Thor's loud chariot
Pass us by

A Sleep Prayer
Now I lay me down to rest
I pray that my home and kin be blessed
Thor guard me through the night
Disir watch over me by starlight
Guardian spirits are always near
and keep me safe, no need to fear
Goodly wights will dance and sing
Happy dreams they always bring
And when I wake to a new day
Sunna's bright sun will light my way

Travel Prayer
Thor keep me safe
Wherever I go
And wherever I am
Your hammer guard me
Thor keep me safe

Poetry is another way to connect to a deity. Similar to prayer it can be useful in contemplation or to reflect on specific qualities of a God. I'm going to include a few poems I have written and one historic poem. I also encourage readers to try writing their own as a way to get closer to Thor.

In Praise of Thor
It seems you believe that
the wisest course is often action --

movement to disperse entropy,
a willingness to fight against any odds,
to wrestle time, to try to drain the sea.
You are not one to hold back
passionate son of Odin,
you do not hesitate, nor waver,
you are decisive in battle,
yet clever enough to seek aid
when it's needed.
Solid as the Earth, your mother,
reliable protector of men,
beloved by the common folk.
Wielding mighty Mjolnir
to good effect,
yet willing to don women's garb
to regain your lost hammer.
Loki's offspring waits for you
patient as the sea,
and when that day comes
you will not turn aside
though destruction awaits you.

Hammer
Around my neck a pendant hangs
silver strung on a strong black cord
shaped like Thor's mighty hammer
worn as a sign to all the world
that I hold true to the old gods
and respect still the ancient ways
I live my life in troth with them
in word and deed for all my days

When I see another wearing
a hammer, intricate or plain

I know the old ways never die
through time and trial they remain
as long as there is anyone who
still calls on the old gods' names
then the strength of their power
in the world is still the same

When my daughters are old enough
I hope they choose to wear with pride
a hammer to show everyone
the faith they find and hold inside
May prayers to the ancient Aesir
lovingly in their hearts shine
shown to the outside world
in a hammer's simple lines

I wanted to include this public domain piece by Henry Wadworth
Longfellow written in 1863:

The Challenge of Thor
I am the God Thor,
I am the War God,
I am the Thunderer!
Here in my Northland,
My fastness and fortress,
Reign I forever!
Here amid icebergs
Rule I the nations;
This is my hammer,
Miölner the mighty;
Giants and sorcerers
Cannot withstand it!

These are the gauntlets

Wherewith I wield it,
And hurl it afar off;
This is my girdle;
Whenever I brace it,
Strength is redoubled!

The light thou beholdest
Stream through the heavens,
In flashes of crimson,
Is but my red beard
Blown by the night-wind,
Affrighting the nations!
Jove is my brother;
Mine eyes are the lightning;
The wheels of my chariot
Roll in the thunder,
The blows of my hammer
Ring in the earthquake!

Force rules the world still,
Has ruled it, shall rule it;
Meekness is weakness,
Strength is triumphant,
Over the whole earth
Still is it Thor's-Day!

Thou art a God too,
O Galilean!
And thus singled-handed
Unto the combat,
Gauntlet or Gospel,
Here I defy thee!

Thor in My Life

I've been involved in Heathenry and the Heathen community since 2006 but I have to admit that my understanding of Thor was always a bit rudimentary. I respected him, honoured him in blóts, kept his image on my altar, and hailed him during thunderstorms but I never really made an effort to understand who Thor really was beyond the surface view the wider community tends to hold of him. It's a comfortable view and there's nothing wrong with it in itself, but it's shallow. It tends to hold Thor as either the Big Brother God or the Tough Warrior God, sometimes a blend of both, but without many nuances. Of course there are people who vary from that and I have had friends who were Thorspeople who undoubtedly had a very complex view of him, but my point here is that my own understanding never went beyond that surface. I was focused on Odin, and somewhat Frau Holle and Berchta, so it was easy to just let myself accept Thor as that popular concept.

It wasn't until I started working on this project that I began to really dig into who Thor was during the Heathen period and who he still is today. And the more I dug into that and saw how deep his worship ran historically and how complex his modern myths are the more I started to see Thor in a new light. He is a mighty warrior God, no doubt, and he is that protective deity that does and has always watched over human kind and our world. But I started to understand that he is also a deity of consecration and oaths, and one who was truly the God of the common man – not in any disparaging sense but in a vital, meaningful one. Thor was in a person's life from conception to the grave and most of the steps in between, in an encompassing way that other deities don't seem to share. There's something beautiful in that which I can appreciate.

End Notes

1 For example in 2015 Vice posted an article titled 'How a

Thor Worshipping Religion Turned Racist' dissecting several Asatru and Odinist groups with racist agendas; it was written in response to the popularity of Marvels Thor. The article can be found here https://www.vice.com/en_us/article/qbxpp5/how-a-thor-worshipping-religion-turned-racist-456 In 2017 The Atlantic ran an article by Sigal Samuel titled 'What to Do When Racists Try to Hijack Your Religion' which took on the subject of white nationalism in Asatru. It can be found here https://www.theatlantic.com/international/archive/2017/11/asatru-heathenry-racism/543864/

2   A better explanation of this and list of common dog whistles you will find in Heathenry can be found online here: https://m.box.com/shared_item/https%3A%2F%2Fapp.box.com%2Fs%2Frfmafp0h7lbcybbi7vjfw8036m2867pd%3Ffbclid%3DIwAR0zGHG_III14n_GIM7-zs8vdQxatWpl7gIACQDG5oVt9mMoXAGEN4E9MOM?fbclid=IwAR1KVcLMEssNyq-MlPqTrxZ2RuYy94K3YiZn8AkMeio_LjO9aTKWhNsYCQA

3   The practice of using wooden carved wooden posts, called God poles, is found in historic Heathenry and has been revived in some modern Heathen practices. These posts or pillars were carved to resemble specific deities and then used as sites for offerings and prayer.

4   A note on meat offerings - Ewing in 'Gods and Worshippers in the Viking and Germanic World' suggests that historically Thor was probably offered goats, which would be killed, cooked into a stew, and shared between offerings to the God and a feast for the people. The practice of animal sacrifice for religious reasons is hotly debated today with some people finding it acceptable if the animal is treated and killed humanely while others feel it is unnecessary and cruel. For those that do eat meat it may be worth considering cooking and sharing a goat dish, with respectfully sourced meat, as an offering. However offering any kind of meat is not required.

Conclusion

Thor is an important deity among the Norse and related cultures for far more than just his giant killing, as essential as that is. Although people might choose to focus on Odin as the head of the pantheon – and perhaps the flashier deity – Thor has always been the more loved and the more universally helpful. He follows the common person throughout life, from birth to death, blessing every stage, even saining land when prayed to. His name and hammer consecrate the runes. He hears and validates oaths and makes marriages and crops fertile. And of course he acts to protect the lives and livelihoods of humans by defending Midgard, our world, against giants and trolls. As Turville-Petre describes him in relation to the Icelanders:

"Thor appears not only as the chief god of the settlers but also as patron and guardian of the settlement itself, of its stability and law." (Turville-Petre, 1964, page 86).

In short he is the ultimate God for anyone to have in their life for nearly any purpose.

Why then is he so often reduced in modern Heathenry to simply a giant killing big brother figure? I suspect that there are several factors in play but that the root of the issue is the way that contemporary American Heathenry grew and the sources it drew on. Historically Thor seems to have gained increasing prominence and popularity into the conversion period in part because he was the deity that came to exemplify the struggle between the old faith against the new. During the 18th and 19th centuries when English speaking poets began to romanticize the pagan Gods, Thor, as demonstrated by his appearances in Longfellow's' poems, was depicted as a warrior and in the German cultural revival of the same period, as we see in Thor's appearance in Wagner's work, he was also reduced to his warrior persona. This continued into the 20th and 21st centuries with his media depictions which have consistently continued to show Thor primarily as a fighter, often brash and reckless. Over this time his nuances and other purviews have increasingly been minimized or ignored. What remains consistent throughout is his connection to thunder and his hammer Mjolnir.

It's true that many who choose Asatru or Heathenry pride themselves on being part of a 'religion with homework' but it's also undeniable that the wider cultural depictions of Thor that we are steeped in do have an effect. If you try to find an image of Thor or search out artwork of him now you are far more likely to see him shown as blond or even with the face of the actor who portrays him in the Marvel movies than shown as mythology describes him: red bearded and large. I have talked to more than one person new to Heathenry who believes, confidently, that Loki is Thor's brother and while this is something that they will undoubtedly eventually realize is from the comics not the Eddas it shows how the popular culture is impacting the spirituality.

For many of us to truly understand who Thor is we need to forget everything we think we knew and begin over. Learn about him with a fresh perspective that encompasses who he was historically and understands where the modern ideas come from. Hopefully this small text has helped to give a reader some idea of Thor's wider scope, or refreshed those who were already familiar with his many purviews among humankind. Thor is not a simple deity, despite how often he may be described that way, but a deeply complex one and we should appreciate all of his layers instead of just the surface.

Appendix

If you have found Thor interesting and would like to dig deeper into who he is you can look at the books in the bibliography for further reading. I would also like to include here some other resource options that might be helpful in a continuing quest to get to know the Thunder God.

Online resources

'Thor the Viking Thunder God' a site by academic D L Ashliman from 1999 which features some basic facts about Thor and links to articles about him http://www.pitt.edu/~dash/thor.html

There is a collection of public domain copies of the Eddas and Sagas on the Sacred Texts website. These are good resources to begin with, especially if budget is an issue, but any translation that comes from that period must be read in its context: translators during the Victorian era tended to omit material they found inappropriate (based on their mores) and to add material that they felt was either needed or made the story more interesting http://www.sacred-texts.com/neu/ice/index.htm

'Thor' on 'Norse Mythology for Smart People' another site with an academic tone and solid references. This entry offers a good concise overview of who Thor is https://norse-mythology. org/gods-and-creatures/the-aesir-gods-and-goddesses/thor/

The Northvegr website is a good source for material on Norse culture http://www.northvegr.net/

The Viking Answer Lady webpage has a good discussion of the 'White Christ versus Red Thor' of the conversion period. It is also a good page in general to use as a resource for more specific questions. http://www.vikinganswerlady.com/hvitkrst.shtml

Music

There is an entire genre of music called Viking Metal which

focuses on Norse themes and mythology and many bands within that and related genres will have songs about or connected to Thor. I can't possibly list them all here but I will offer some highlights to give readers some ideas of where to start.

Swedish Death Metal band, Amon Amarth, has an album titled 'Twilight of the Thunder God' and much of their music deals with themes around Norse mythology.

The Polish Metal band, Hazael, has an album out titled 'Thor'.

The Faroese Metal band, Týr, has a song called 'Hammer of Thor' which tells the story of the forging of the hammer

The Norwegian Metal band, Wardruna, also covers Norse mythology themes in their music.

And of course there is always the classic: Wagner's 'Das Rheingold' opera can be found in multiple formats and is also available on Youtube.

Statues

Dryad Design offers three different Thor statue options, one a smaller figurine and two slightly larger seated figures. One seated figure is flanked by his two goats, the other holds his hammer in his lap. They were all originally hand craved by artist Paul Borda then cast in resin and the detail carries through.

Sacred Source has a plaque featuring Thor riding in his chariot and a museum replica statue of Thor holding a hammer in his lap.

There is also a wholesaling company that makes a more dramatic statue, styled after idealized Viking imagery, that can be found in many retailers who carry deity statues. If none of these suit your taste there are a variety of hand carved or moulded options on sites like Etsy that can be made to order, although I do advise caution and some research before purchasing direct from artists; some are known to have ties to white supremacy groups.

Bibliography

Adalsteinsson, J., (1999). Under the Cloak: a Pagan Ritual Turning Point in the Conversion of Iceland

--- (1998). A Piece of Horse Liver: Myth, Ritual and Folklore in Old Icelandic Sources

Adam of Bremen (1876) Gesta Hammaburgensis ecclesiae pontificum

Arnold, M., (2011) Thor: Myth to Marvel

Barrett, J., (2008). "*The Norse in Scotland*"; The Viking World.

Bauschatz, P., (1982) The Well and the Tree

Bellows, H., (1936) The Poetic Edda

Birley, A., (1999) Tacitus Agricola and Germany

Byock, J., (1998) The Saga of King Hrolf Kraki

--- (2005). The Prose Edda

Clements, J., (2005) The Vikings

Cook, R., (2001). Njal's Saga

Colm (2013) Thor's Wood, A Sacred Grove Near Viking Age Dublin? Retrieved from irisharchaeology.ie/2013/07/thors-wood-a-sacred-grove-in-viking-dublin/

Crawford, B., (1987) Scandinavian Scotland

Crossley-Holland, K., (1980) The Norse Myths

Dasent, G., (2001) Popular Tales from Norse Mythology

D'Aulaires, I., and D'Aulaires E., (1967). D'Aulaires' Book of Norse Myths

Downham, C., (2007) Viking Kings of Britain and Ireland: The Dynasty of Ívarr to A.D. 1014

Dumézil, G., (1973) Gods of the Ancient Northmen

Ellis Davidson, H., (1964) Gods and Myths of Northern Europe

--- (1965) "Thor's Hammer". Folklore vol 76 issue 1

--- (1968) The Road to Hel

--- (1988) Myths and Symbols in Pagan Europe: Early Scandinavian and Celtic Religions

--- (1993) The Lost Beliefs of Northern Europe

Ewing, T., (2008). Gods and Worshippers in the Viking and Germanic World

Fischer, L., (2012). Evidence of Vikings by County. Retrieved from http://www.vikingage.mic.ul.ie/resource_vikings-by-county.html

Fisher, P., (1980) Saxo Grammaticus: The History of the Danes Books I-IX

Fortson, B., (2004). Indo-European language and culture: an introduction

Graham-Campbell, J., and Batey, C., (1998) Vikings in Scotland: An Archaeological Survey

Grimm, J., (1888) Teutonic Mythology volume 1

Gundarsson, K., ed. (2006) Our Troth volume 1 History and Lore

Herbert, K., (1995). Looking for the Lost gods of England

Heyl, J (1897) Volkssagen, Bräuche und Meinungen aus Tirol

Hollander, L., (2007) Heimskringla

Larrington, C., (1996) The Poetic Edda

Lindow, J., (2001) Norse Mythology: A Guide to the Gods, Heroes, Rituals, and Beliefs

Magoun, F., (1949) 'On the Old-Germanic Altar or Oath Ring'; Acta Philogica Scandinavica

McNeill, F., (1961) The Silver Bough, volume 3

Ó Corráin, D., (1998) Vikings in Ireland and Scotland in the Ninth Century

--- (2008) "The Vikings and Ireland"; The Viking World

O'Donoghue, H., (2008) From Asgard to Valhalla

Pálsson, H., and Edwards, P., (1981). Orkneyinga Saga

Pollington, S., (2003). The Mead-Hall: Feasting in Anglo-Saxon England

Preet, E., (2010) Slainte! Ireland's Viking Heritage. Retrieved from http://www.irishcentral.com/IrishAmerica/Irelands-Viking-Heritage-110976559.html

Samuel, S., (2017) 'What To Do When Racists Try To Hijack Your Religion', the Atlantic. Retrieved from https://www.

theatlantic.com/international/archive/2017/11/asatru-heath
enry-racism/543864/

Scudder, B., (1997). Egil's Saga

Sheehan, J. and Ó Corráin, D., (2010) 'The Viking Age: Ireland and
the West'. Proceedings of the Fifteenth Viking Congress

Sigrdrifumal   http://www.northvegr.org/the%20eddas/the%2
0poetic%20edda%20%20-%20thorpe%20translation/
sigrdrifumal%20-%20the%20lay%20of%20sigrdrifa%20
page%201.html

Simek, R., (1993) Dictionary of Northern Mythology

Thorpe, B., (1851). Northern Mythology, Compromising the
Principal Traditions and Superstitions of Scandinavia, North
Germany, and the Netherlands

Towrie, S., (2019). "Dian-stanes and 'Thunderstones'"; Orkneyjar.
Retrieved from   http://www.orkneyjar.com/tradition/dian.
htm

Turville-Petre, E., (1964) Myth and Religion of the North: The
Religion of Ancient Scandinavia

Viking Answer Lady (2012). Vikings in Ireland. Retrieved from
http://www.vikinganswerlady.com/Ireland.shtml

Woolf, A., (2009) Scandinavian Scotland – Twenty Years After

Other Titles by Morgan Daimler

Brigid
Meeting the Celtic Goddess of Poetry, Forge, and Healing Well
978-1-78535-320-8 (paperback)
978-1-78535-321-5 (e-book)

~~~~~~~~~~~~~~~~~

Gods and Goddesses of Ireland
A Guide to Irish Deities
978-1-78279-315-1 (paperback)
978-1-78535-450-2 (e-book)

~~~~~~~~~~~~~~~~~

Irish Paganism
Meeting the Celtic God of Wave and Wonder
978-1-78535-145-7 (paperback)
978-1-78535-146-4 (e-book)

~~~~~~~~~~~~~~~~~

Manannán mac Lir
Meeting the Celtic God of Wave and Wonder
978-1-78535-810-4 (paperback)
978-1-78535-811-1 (e-book)

~~~~~~~~~~~~~~~~~

Odin
Meeting the Norse Allfather
978-1-78535-480-9 (paperback)
978-1-78535-481-6 (e-book)

The Dagda
Meeting the Good God of Ireland
978-1-78535-640-7 (paperback)
978-1-78535-641-4 (e-book)

~~~~~~~~~~~~~~~~~~

The Morrigan
Meeting the Great Queens
978-1-78279-833-0 (paperback)
978-1-78279-834-7 (e-book)

~~~~~~~~~~~~~~~~~~

A New Dictionary of Fairies
A 21st Century Exploration of Celtic and Related Western European Fairies
978-1-78904-036-4 (paperback)
978-1-78904-037-1 (e-book)

~~~~~~~~~~~~~~~~~~

Fairies
A Guide to the Celtic Fair Folk
978-1-78279-650-3 (paperback)
978-1-78279-696-1 (e-book)

~~~~~~~~~~~~~~~~~~

Fairycraft
Following the Path of Fairy Witchcraft
978-1-78535-051-1 (paperback)
978-1-78535-052-8 (e-book)

Fairy Queens

Meeting the Queens of the Otherworld

978-1-78535-833-3 (paperback)

978-1-78535-842-5 (e-book)

~~~~~~~~~~~~~~~~~

Fairy Witchcraft

A Neopagan's Guide to the Celtic Fairy Faith

978-1-78279-343-4 (paperback)

978-1-78279-344-1 (e-book)

~~~~~~~~~~~~~~~~~

Travelling the Fairy Path

Experiencing the myth, magic, and mysticism of Fairy Witchcraft

978-1-78535-752-7 (paperback)

978-1-78535-753-4 (e-book)

MOON
BOOKS

PAGANISM & SHAMANISM

What is Paganism? A religion, a spirituality, an alternative belief system, nature worship? You can find support for all these definitions (and many more) in dictionaries, encyclopaedias, and text books of religion, but subscribe to any one and the truth will evade you. Above all Paganism is a creative pursuit, an encounter with reality, an exploration of meaning and an expression of the soul. Druids, Heathens, Wiccans and others, all contribute their insights and literary riches to the Pagan tradition. Moon Books invites you to begin or to deepen your own encounter, right here, right now.

If you have enjoyed this book, why not tell other readers by posting a review on your preferred book site.

Recent bestsellers from Moon Books are:

Journey to the Dark Goddess
How to Return to Your Soul
Jane Meredith
Discover the powerful secrets of the Dark Goddess and
transform your depression, grief and pain into healing
and integration.
Paperback: 978-1-84694-677-6 ebook: 978-1-78099-223-5

Shamanic Reiki
Expanded Ways of Working with Universal Life Force Energy
Llyn Roberts, Robert Levy
Shamanism and Reiki are each powerful ways of healing; together,
their power multiplies. *Shamanic Reiki* introduces techniques to
help healers and Reiki practitioners tap ancient healing wisdom.
Paperback: 978-1-84694-037-8 ebook: 978-1-84694-650-9

Pagan Portals – The Awen Alone
Walking the Path of the Solitary Druid
Joanna van der Hoeven
An introductory guide for the solitary Druid, *The Awen Alone* will
accompany you as you explore, and seek out your own place
within the natural world.
Paperback: 978-1-78279-547-6 ebook: 978-1-78279-546-9

A Kitchen Witch's World of Magical Herbs & Plants
Rachel Patterson
A journey into the magical world of herbs and plants, filled with
magical uses, folklore, history and practical magic. By popular
writer, blogger and kitchen witch, Tansy Firedragon.
Paperback: 978-1-78279-621-3 ebook: 978-1-78279-620-6

Medicine for the Soul
The Complete Book of Shamanic Healing
Ross Heaven
All you will ever need to know about shamanic healing and how to
become your own shaman...
Paperback: 978-1-78099-419-2 ebook: 978-1-78099-420-8

Shaman Pathways – The Druid Shaman
Exploring the Celtic Otherworld
Danu Forest
A practical guide to Celtic shamanism with exercises and
techniques as well as traditional lore for exploring the Celtic
Otherworld.
Paperback: 978-1-78099-615-8 ebook: 978-1-78099-616-5

Traditional Witchcraft for the Woods and Forests
A Witch's Guide to the Woodland with Guided Meditations and
Pathworking
Melusine Draco
A Witch's guide to walking alone in the woods, with guided
meditations and pathworking.
Paperback: 978-1-84694-803-9 ebook: 978-1-84694-804-6

Wild Earth, Wild Soul
A Manual for an Ecstatic Culture
Bill Pfeiffer
Imagine a nature-based culture so alive and so connected,
spreading like wildfire. This book is the first flame...
Paperback: 978-1-78099-187-0 ebook: 978-1-78099-188-7

Naming the Goddess
Trevor Greenfield
Naming the Goddess is written by over eighty adherents and
scholars of Goddess and Goddess Spirituality.
Paperback: 978-1-78279-476-9 ebook: 978-1-78279-475-2

Shapeshifting into Higher Consciousness
Heal and Transform Yourself and Our World with Ancient
Shamanic and Modern Methods
Llyn Roberts
Ancient and modern methods that you can use every day to
transform yourself and make a positive difference in the world.
Paperback: 978-1-84694-843-5 ebook: 978-1-84694-844-2

Readers of ebooks can buy or view any of these bestsellers by
clicking on the live link in the title. Most titles are published in
paperback and as an ebook. Paperbacks are available in traditional
bookshops. Both print and ebook formats are available online.

Find more titles and sign up to our readers' newsletter at
http://www.johnhuntpublishing.com/paganism
Follow us on Facebook at https://www.facebook.com/MoonBooks
and Twitter at https://twitter.com/MoonBooksJHP